POISON ARROWS

POISON ARROWS

North American Indian Hunting and Warfare

By David E. Jones

UNIVERSITY OF TEXAS PRESS   AUSTIN

Requests for permission to reproduce material from
this work should be sent to:
Permissions
University of Texas Press
P.O. Box 7819
Austin, TX 78713-7819
www.utexas.edu/utpress/about/bpermission.html

⊗ The paper used in this book meets the minimum
requirements of ANSI/NISO Z39.48-1992 (R1997)
(Permanence of Paper).

Library of Congress Cataloging-in-Publication Data

Jones, David E.
  Poison arrows : North American Indian hunting
and warfare / by David E. Jones — 1st ed.
      p.   cm.
  Includes bibliographical references and index.
  ISBN: 0-292-72229-X

    1. Indian weapons—North America.   2. Indians
of North America—Ethnobotany.   3. Indians of
North America—Hunting.   4. Arrow poisons—
North America.   5. Poisonous plants—North
America.   6. Poisonous animals—North America.
7. Neurotoxic agents—North America.   I. Title.
    E98.A65J65   2006
    355.8'2—dc22
                                            2006024691

Contents

Disclaimer

THIS IS A work of ethnography and ethnobotany, not of toxicology.

The material presented is based on oral reports of North American Indians concerning their knowledge and uses of poisons, particularly those with military applications. With but a few exceptions, this information has not been tested under laboratory conditions. It is rightly considered poison lore, an aspect of hunting, warfare, and martial cultural knowledge transmitted through generations by Native Americans.

THE PLANTS DISCUSSED IN THIS BOOK SHOULD NOT BE HANDLED OR INGESTED EXCEPT UNDER THE GUIDANCE OF EXPERTS!

Acknowledgments

I WOULD LIKE to thank my wife Jane for her support and skillful editing during the writing of this work. I could not have done it without her. Likewise, I owe a debt of gratitude to Ida Cook, Wayne Van Horne, and David Butler for comments on the evolving draft, and to Theresa May, editor-in-chief at the University of Texas Press, for her faith in this project.

Introduction

THE LATE TWENTIETH and early twenty-first centuries have witnessed a renewed concern among nations of the world regarding the use of biological and chemical weapons of war, especially by terrorists and so-called rogue nations. The fact that all major nations possess extensive weapons laboratories and production facilities, combined with events of the past several decades, illustrates that anxiety over these weapons is firmly based in reality.

In 1968 at Dugway, Utah, a laboratory testing an extremely toxic agent precipitated a chemical cloud that killed 6,000 sheep. The plant was later closed. An accidental release of aerosol in 1979 from Compound 19, a biological weapons plant in Sverdlovsk, Russia, killed sixty-six people who were directly downwind. On April 26, 1986, at the Chernobyl Nuclear Power Station in the Republic of Belarus, a reactor mishap released approximately seventy radioactive substances, affecting to some extent almost the entire population of the republic and forcing the evacuation of 24,000.

More ominous than accidental assaults are intentional applications of biological and chemical agents. In 1988, the Iraqi government attacked the Kurdish village of Birjinni with the nerve agent sarin, killing hundreds of innocent men, women, and children. In the 1980s, chemical weapons were reported in Laos, Cambodia, Afghanistan, Iran, and Iraq. In 1995, the Aum Shinri Kyo cult released sarin in Tokyo's subway system during rush hour, injuring 5,500 and killing 11. Americans were terrorized in 2001 and 2002 with the specter of anthrax-tainted mail moving through the postal system, and in January 2003, several men were arrested for producing ricin, a poison more deadly than sarin, in a small apartment in London. In 1997, then Secretary of Defense William Cohen singled out Libya, Iran, Iraq, and Syria as countries aggressively seeking nuclear, biological, and chemical weapons.

It is safe to say that the threat of biological and chemical weapons against the U.S. military and civilian population is greater now than at any other time in our nation's history. Unlike military hardware, which can cost millions of dollars and can require large production facilities with highly trained staff, these weapons are relatively inexpensive and easy to produce in small spaces. They are difficult to detect and could, if used with tactical expertise, kill many of an enemy population, military and civilian alike.

Appearing to be growing in its potential menace, poison warfare can be defined as employing toxic agents to kill, injure, or impair an enemy combatant. Biological warfare employs living organisms—most commonly disease microorganisms such as the spore-forming bacterium *Bacillus anthracis* (Anthrax) and the contagious febrile (fever) smallpox virus to threaten men, animals, or plants.

Chemical warfare kills or impairs the enemy with poisonous corrosives, smoke, mists, and asphyxiating gas, with the most modern form being radioactivity. Some, chlorine gas for example, must be inhaled whereas others, such as mustard gas, need only touch the skin. Many—poisoned arrows, darts, spear points, or knives—must be injected. Both chemical and biological warfare are tactical and neither is suited for the large-scale battlefield, although modern military technology is rapidly solving the problem of wide-ranging deployment.

Chemicals in warfare date to 1000 BC when the Chinese dispersed arsenical smoke in battle. Six hundred years later, the Spartans fought the Athenian-allied cities during the Peloponnesian War with "beam smoke" (formula unknown), and Scythian archers dipped their war arrows in blood, manure, and decomposing bodies. In the sixth century BC, the Assyrians poisoned their enemy's drinking water with rye ergot. During the siege of Krissa in the same century, Solon used the poisonous herb hellebore in a similar attack. When Hannibal attacked the ships of Pegamus at Eurymedon in 190 BC, he ordered poisonous snakes thrown onto the enemy's decks prior to attempts at boarding.

Plague spread among the defenders of Kaffa (present-day Feodosia in Crimea) in 1346 when attackers hurled infected corpses over the city walls. In 1710, the Russians used the same tactic against the Swedish army. Polish artillery general Siemenowics filled hollow canister shells with the saliva of rabid dogs and fired them against his adversaries in 1650.

In the fifteenth century, Francisco Pizarro gave contaminated blankets to the native populations he encountered in South America, and Sir Jeffrey Amherst distributed smallpox-laden blankets to Indians loyal to the French during the French and Indian War (1756–1763). The resulting epidemic led to the loss of Fort Carillon to the English.

In 1855, when the British and Russians were bogged down in trench warfare, Sir Lyon Playfair proposed to the British high command that they place cyanide in artillery shells and shoot them into the Russian ranks. His suggestion was rejected as inhumane. Using a rationale that would appear from time to time in future discussions on the morality of chemical warfare, he argued for its civility, noting that the doomed enemy would die quickly.

Modern chemical warfare traces its history to World War I and one man, Dr. Fritz Haber, a Nobel laureate and world-famous chemist who had developed a process for extracting nitrates from the atmosphere to produce fertilizers and explosives. He came to understand that the poisonous by-products of his chemical research could have military significance. He experimented with numerous agents before fixing upon chlorine, but when he suggested it as a weapon to the German high command, they turned him away, calling the use of poison gas ungentlemanly. They shifted their position in 1915 when they found themselves stalemated in trench warfare on the western front. Haber was granted an officer's rank and instructed to organize a chemical corps.

The first chlorine gas attack took place April 22, 1915, against French and Algerian troops dug in at Ypres, Belgium. When the Germans released 180 kilograms of the gas, it stripped the linings from soldiers' lungs, causing them to drown in their own fluids. Two days later, the Germans attacked Canadian lines with similar results. In two days of fighting, five thousand Allies were killed and ten thousand more disabled, many of them permanently.

By late 1915, the Germans had developed phosgene gas, an agent ten times more deadly than chlorine. The Allies, not far behind, accelerated their own chemical programs. The French and Germans were exchanging toxin-filled artillery shells in 1916, and the British added large-scale gas barrages the following year.

Livens Projectors, three-foot-long metal tubes first used in battle by the British in 1917, were positioned in the ground at a forty-five-degree angle. Each tube held a thirty-pound canister of gas—in this case, phosgene—and was armed and fired electrically. The cylinders could reach almost a mile, and their impact triggered a small discharge that exploded the tubes. During the system's debut, the British fired 2,340 canisters, releasing nearly fifty tons of liquid phosgene that instantly vaporized into clouds of poisonous gas. The Livens Projectors granted a temporary edge to the British in gas warfare, but soon the Germans countered with mustard gas, which was designed to attack exposed skin.

Approximately 113,000 tons of chemical weapons were used in World War I, killing some 92,000 men and wounding 1.3 million. The chemical aspects of the warfare were so devastating that the hostile nations of World War II were loath to use it; however, during this time the Germans developed tabun, sarin, and soman—three of the most deadly chemical weapons ever created.

The preceding abbreviated overview of Western military chemical warfare was recounted conventionally.[1] True to the conceit of the West that its culture was modeled after that of the Ancients, most Western military historians cite them (classical Greeks and Romans) before focusing on Western European history. Are we to believe that only the Greeks, Romans, and a few kingdoms of the Near East used poisons in warfare? The anthropological record clearly refutes this impression. In fact, from the dawn of recorded history, humans worldwide have possessed detailed knowledge of how to kill with chemicals.

I became interested in non-Western chemical warfare while pursuing research on native North American armor, shields, and fortifications.[2] In almost every case in which armor was used by North American Indian groups, they were fighting enemies who had poisoned arrows. Because armor was found from the Bering Straits to the Southeast and from Canada to New Mexico, chemical poisons likewise had a wide distribution.

Most reports I encountered, however, claimed that poisoned arrows were neither important, common, nor effective. One source states that "[t]here were but a few tribes that used poisoned arrows. The poisoning of arrows was not generally popular among the natives of North America."[3] Another comments that "[p]oisoned arrows were not so widely used by the Indians as is commonly assumed from the exaggerated accounts of the Spanish conquistadors."[4] And another says that "the narrative accounts by early explorers from the Florida tribes northward to the Great Lakes have treated arrow poisoning so casually that speculative reasoning has not been swayed to the affirmative by the few references given ... previously. The subject has been treated only briefly and with considerable hesitation."[5] Others cite references but remain doubtful of the ubiquity of the practice.

Some of the early reporters seem ambivalent and even contradictory about the presence and efficacy of poisoned arrows.[6] One such account begins with a description of a cavalry mount that had been shot with a poisoned arrow by a Navaho warrior. "He swelled up enormously, evidently suffered much pain, and died in the course of a night, certainly from the effects of a poison, as the wound inflicted by the arrow was not mortal, neither from its seat or its severity. Of course, a wound of this nature, if it involves parts beyond reach of knife or cautery, is fatal."[7] However, the account continues, "Strange to say such arrows are of infrequent use. Among some seventy-six cases of arrow wounds received from Navaho, Apache, and Utah Indians, we have seen no case of poisoned arrow wounds in the human subject, nor have we heard of such a case after careful inquiry."

An observer writes of the Indians of California, "[H]ere I may mention, no arrow-poison; but I have known some of the California Indians to get a rattlesnake, and irritate it until it had repeatedly struck into the liver of some animal, impregnating it with its virus. They would then dip their arrows into this poisoned mess."[8]

One commentator dismisses the issue of poisoned arrows: "The arrowheads used by Native Americans against each other and against newcomers occasionally carried poisons but they really didn't need to. The Indians were such skilled bowmen that any enhancement to the basics was normally unnecessary. The toxic effect of 'poisoned-tipped' arrows has always been overplayed by Hollywood, so much so that contaminated arrowheads have become an essential ingredient in the collective consciousness of the West. Such is the power of the modern media."[9]

The report continues: "The Indians' use of viscera from all types of animals as the poisoning agent is the stuff of legend. One band of Apaches, the Lipans, dipped their arrows into the sap of the Yucca, which they thought was very poisonous. According to the natives, the points of the Yucca possess a mystic power that will adversely affect anyone hit by an arrow dipped in its sap."[10] The author perhaps alludes to the Lipan Apache belief in the toxicity of Yucca tips as stemming from the so-called Doctrine of Signatures, found in the belief systems of many cultures, where every medicinal plant has a "sign" that reveals its therapeutic properties. Thus, the Zuni, for example, use the root of a plant they call *hoktdidasha* (cougar) because of its resemblance to a cougar's tail. In this case, the animal's strength and appearance suggest the medicinal value of the plant. A plant with a long, twisted root may be seen as suitable to treat snakebite; dandelions, because of their color, might be considered efficacious in the treatment of jaundice; and the needle-sharp spines of the Yucca denote its value as a poison.

Some authors who deny the existence or effectiveness of Indian war poisons offer as proof the chanting and magico-religious ritual behavior associated in some tribes with its manufacture. Most societies, however, precede a dangerous endeavor with some type of group repetition of essential principles to which they must adhere for the sake of safety or success. This does not define the undertaking as fraudulent. A particular code of procedure chanted prior to a perilous activity serves to reinforce safe behavior and coordinate the behavior of participants.

An army surgeon wrote of an Apache poisoned-arrow wound that was "a mere scratch upon the upper portion of the scapula, but previous to death the flesh fell from the back as far down as the nates, exposing at various points the ribs and spinal process."[11] That horrific description should have impressed the author, who, after quoting the surgeon, claimed that the Apache believed that their poisoned points had only a "mystical power."

Other authorities were woefully uninformed. An author of a surgical textbook states that the Paiutes were the only tribe of North American Indians who poisoned their arrows, and another reports, "There is no record of any California Indians using poisons to take human life, for murder, or to kill off their enemies."[12] A body of literature, however, cites the use of poison arrows by California tribes, including citations on a number of plants with which they poisoned their arrows for hunting and warfare.[13]

A novel dismissal of poison arrows is found in a letter from John Clayton, a minister at Jamestown between 1684 and 1686, to his friend Dr. Jeremiah Grew about the medical practices of the Virginia Indians:

> But any herbs wherewith they poison their darts I never could
> hear specify'd. And as persons engaged in long marches are liable
> to many accidents which may contribute to an ill state of health,

when a slight wound in battle has often proved mortal this I apprehend to have been the cause why the physician has rather chosen to attribute the death of his patient to the dart, than the want of skill in himself.[14]

By ignoring three bodies of information, the preceding authors have added to the confusion surrounding North American Indian biological and chemical warfare. A reasonable approach to the subject must include an exhaustive study of North American Indian ethnobotany (with an eye toward knowledge of poisons); a worldwide sample of poison-arrow use to evaluate North American Indians in a global perspective; and a contemporary and wide-ranging appreciation of North American Indian warfare, weapons, and tactics. Information gleaned from these areas will demonstrate that at the time of contact, poison arrows were found in all culture areas of Native North America, and they were quite effective in warfare.

Gathering substantive information proved difficult for a number of reasons. Most accounts indicate that poison making was, with few exceptions, limited to certain men; women, in the main, were not privy to this knowledge. Because only a few people in a particular group could offer expert commentary on the existence and nature of the practice, the avenues for investigators were limited.

Further, as with armor use by North American Indians, only a brief period existed when poison-arrow usage could be catalogued. Both armor and poison arrows disappeared at about the same time and for the same reason: the acquisition of efficient high-caliber repeating rifles by Indian and non-Indian communities.

The record is impeded by the types of researchers who were in a position to study poison arrows at the time of contact. Most were untrained in anything resembling ethnobotany and had little desire to investigate warfare patterns where poison-arrow making would be found.

Attitudes about poison held by contact and postcontact Indians also cloud the record. For example, the Chiricahua Apache thought poisons were the special province of witches, a belief common to many Indian groups. An Apache ethnographer wrote,

Chiricahua Apache do not like to discuss the topic of witchcraft. Some informants who were willing to talk about anything else, even the most intimate matters, simply refused to give information on this subject. There are a number of reasons for this. In the first place, to demonstrate too much knowledge of witchcraft places a person under suspicion of being a witch himself, too great a familiarity with the ways of those who "kill in secret" is considered a result of unhealthy interest or dubious practices. Also, to speak freely about witches is to invite their attention and persecution, especially of the comments, as those of any decent Apache should be critical.[15]

At the time of French contact, Huron poison making was associated with sorcerers, and "anyone catching them was authorized by the consent of the whole country to cleave their skulls, without fear of being called to account."[16] Often, Indian writers connected the use of poison with Satanic influences. A California Indian commented,

Being a poisonous plant, the poppy fields *Eschscholzia californica*, [California Poppy] were of no use to the good morals and medical practices of the Indian doctors in the days gone by. But the notorious witch-doctor, having more of the devil in him than of anything else, made general use of this plant to compound some of his poisonous medicines in his irregular and evil practice.[17]

A native Ojibway speaker wrote,

According to other accounts, the dispersion of the Ojibway from the island of their refuge was sudden and entire. The Evil Spirit had found a strong foothold amongst them. It is said by my informants that the medicine men of this period had come to a knowledge of the most subtle poisons, and they revenged the least affront with certain death. It is said that if a young woman refused the addresses of one of these medicine men, she fell a victim of his poison and her body being disinterred was feasted on by the horrid murderer. The Ojibways, at this period, fell entirely under the power of their Satanic medicine men.[18]

Beliefs about poisoning and an aura of evil and fear surrounding the manufacture of poisons impeded access to pertinent knowledge concerning the practice. Further, Indian experts were few and often un-willing to admit to their expertise, particular to non-Indians. But despite the difficulties, it is possible to present a relatively large body of infor-mation on the use of poisons by North American Indians. In fact, that such a body of knowledge is scattered through ethnobotanical materials and early-contact sources suggests that, if the above factors had not been in place, the data on the subject would be far richer.

POISON ARROWS

Chapter 1

On Plant Poisons

What makes a plant poisonous? What effects do poisons delivered by arrow, spear point, knife, or dart have on the victim? Answers to these questions are not as clear-cut as one might think. Botanist Edward R. Ricciuti wrote,

> How many species are capable of poisoning people? No one really knows. The toxic properties of hundreds, even thousands, of species may await discovery, and inclusion in the medical literature. The poisons in many common plants may be undetected simply because no one ever has eaten them, or if someone has, the symptoms of poisoning never have been linked to the plants.
>
> The common wisteria exemplifies the on-going discovery of poisonous plants. This woody vine with its cascading blossoms grows in gardens all over the world, but only in 1961 was it discovered that ingesting its pea-like seeds causes severe stomach poisoning.[1]

The plethora of known poisonous plants and the continuing discovery of those once thought to be chemically passive may clarify conflicting opinions between Native Americans and non–Indian botanists. The succeeding chapters cite plants believed by Native Americans to be poisonous, regardless of the lack of confirmation by modern botanists, for North American Indians had a much more intimate relationship with the flora of their world than contemporary botanists, and for tens of thousands of years longer.

Poisonous plants grow throughout the world and do not seem to be environmentally bound. They appear in most plant families and are so widely and randomly distributed in the plant kingdom that no botanical grouping can be defined exclusively on the basis of poisonous qualities.

Plant poisons number in the hundreds, but generally one or more compounds from a handful of major chemical groups account for the toxicity. Of these, the most important is the alkaloids, complicated organic compounds characterized by the nitrogen they contain.[2]

Plant chemicals with medicinal value, phytochemicals, are secondary metabolites, a class of chemicals not required for plant activities such as photosynthesis. Most often defensive in nature, secondary metabolites provide plants the nauseous or toxic chemicals to ward off predators.

Alkaloids, of which there are thousands, form the largest group of phytochemicals, with about 10 percent of them occurring in flowering plants. They appear in certain mushrooms and mosses, as well as in a limited number of animals, such as beaver and spotted salamander. The most powerful ingredients in strychnine, caffeine, nicotine, opium, and curare, they generate the hallucinogenic effect of LSD and peyote, the latter comprising thirteen narcotic alkaloids, including mescaline.

Poisonous plants also contain glycosides, resins, and acids. Glycosides are carbohydrates whose poisonous by-products include cyanide, digitalis, and one of the several toxic compounds in solanine, the poison in nightshade, the most notorious of the *Solanaceae*. The danger in Jack in the Pulpit, for example, is an acid whereas the toxic "milk" of the milkweed is a resin.[3]

Most ingredients in arrow poisoning were floral in nature, but many societies incorporated insects and animals or animal products, such as scorpions, poisonous ants, spiders, caterpillars, snake venom, and decayed animal organs. Plant poisons exercise their toxic effects through the action of alkaloids, acids, glycosides, and resins, but the poisons derived from animal products generally induce gas gangrene, tetanus, and severe infection because of the presence of those spores in decaying animal matter. Bacterial flora in the mouths and venom glands of poisonous snakes is a crucial factor in understanding snakebite poisoning. "Overwhelming bacterial infections secondary to snakebite wounds frequently produce morbidity and mortality when the venom alone would not have been sufficiently toxic to do so. Poisonous snakebite wounds have been described as contaminated venom-laden, anaerobic puncture wounds, which predispose to infection and tissue destruction."[4] Significantly, many tribes treated arrows with the rapidly acting plant poisons for hunting and those for war with animal poisons.

Snake venom as an arrow poison is widely known. Dozens of North

American Indian groups applied rattlesnake venom, alone or as an ingredient in a complex recipe, to their arrows. Bushmen in southwest Africa mix a resin extracted from the root of *Buphane toxicaria* (Ox-bane) with the venom of the ringhals that, on the fingernail-sized heads of their arrows, can with one shot kill large game animals over a period of several hours. Another venom-based African poison is concocted from puff adders and crushed beetles, plants, and resins. In eastern India, Bengali tribesmen tie small wads of cotton soaked in cobra venom to the tips of their arrows.[5]

Although Native Americans used a great variety of plant products (roots, flowers, seeds, twigs, fruits) as poisons, they considered *Cicuta spp.* (Water Hemlock), *Datura spp.* (Sacred Thornapple), *Veratrum viride* (American False Hellebore), and *Aconitum spp.* (Monkshood) the most poisonous.

The major species of *Cicuta* used by North American Indians—*C. masculata, C. occidentalis, C. virosa,* and *C. douglasii*—exude a yellow, res-inous substance called cicutoxin, a highly unsaturated higher alcohol that acts on the central nervous system. Its effects provide it the distinction of being the most poisonous plant genus in North America. It permeates the plant but is most concentrated in the root, and a piece the size of a pea can kill a man.

Within fifteen to thirty minutes of ingesting *Cicuta* root, the victim experiences sharp stomach pains, vomiting, rapid pulse, dilated pupils, dizziness, diarrhea, and finally convulsions so powerful that he or she often bites off the tongue and shatters teeth. Death comes from respiratory failure after complete paralysis. Thirty to 50 percent of *Cicuta* poisoning leads to death.

Cicutoxin poisoning has at times resulted from mistaking *Cicuta* for artichokes, celery, sweet potatoes, sweet anise, wild ginseng, or water parsnip. Since record keeping began in 1900, one death per year has been attributed to this plant. Anecdotal accounts suggest how quickly it can kill.[6] A fisherman in Kentucky confused *C. masculata* and wild parsnips, and a few bites of the root resulted in convulsions thirty minutes later. A French soldier drank soup to which *Cicuta* had been accidentally added and was dead three hours later. In another case, a man mistook *C. masculata* for parsley and lived only fifteen minutes after ingesting it.

Datura belongs to the nightshade family, that of tobacco, tomatoes, hot peppers, potatoes, and eggplants. Species used by Native Americans include *Datura wrightii* (Sacred Thornapple or Southwestern Thornapple), *D. meteloides* (Sacred Datura), *D. stramonium* (Jimson Weed), and *D. Inoxia* (Toloache) with *D. stramonium* more prevalent in the East and *D. meteloides* in the West.

Datura is extremely toxic. The Centers for Disease Control and Prevention reports that 89 percent of *Datura* usage results in poisoning, four to five grams of leaf proving fatal to a child. In an adult, as little as half a teaspoon of crushed seeds will produce complete delirium followed by weeks of disorientation, and ingestion of a mere twenty seeds is lethal. The poisonous solanaceous alkaloids (tropane configuration)—including atropine, hyoscamine (isomeric with atropine) and hyoscine (scopolamine)—cause intense thirst, visual disturbances from the atropine that can last from six hours to three weeks, flushed skin, central nervous system hyperirritability, delirium, rapid heartbeat, elevated temperature, violent hallucinations, convulsions, and coma leading to death.

The story of *D. stramonium*'s popular name, Jimson Weed or Jamestown Weed, offers a dramatic description of poisoning. The account, written in 1705 by Robert Beverly, describes events in 1676 when soldiers were sent to Jamestown, Virginia, to quell elements of the Bacon rebellion. They were served soup, which was accidentally spiced with *D. stramonium*.

> Some of them eat plentifully of it, the effect of which was a very pleasant comedy for they turned into fools upon it for several days. One would blow up a feather in the air; another would dart straws at it with much fury; another, stark naked, was sitting in a corner, like a monkey, grinning and making faces at them; a fourth would fondly kiss and paw his companions and sneer in their faces with a countenance more antic than any Dutch Droll. A thousand such simple tricks they played and after eleven days, returned to themselves again, not remembering anything that had passed.[7]

Many American Indian groups considered *Veratrum viride* (American False Hellebore) and *V. californicum* (California False Hellebore) highly toxic. *V. viride* possesses sixty toxic steroidal alkaloids, the most potent being jervine, cyclopamine, cycloposine, pseudo-jervine, cevadine, rubijervine, and veratralbine. Jervine depresses circulation and the central nervous system and irritates motor centers in the brain, causing convulsions. Veratralbine slows the pulse rate, lowers blood pressure, and impedes respiration. Hellebore roots are five to ten times more poisonous than the leaves or the stems. Symptoms of poisoning include extreme muscular weakness, frequent nausea and vomiting, cold and clammy skin, giddiness, and impaired vision. A powerful cardiac and spinal depressant, Hellebore can paralyze the heart muscle and cause fatality.

Various species of *Aconitum,* including *Aconitum columbianum* (Columbian Monkshood), produce aconitines, a group of toxic alkaloids. The scientific name derives from the Greek word for "dart" and suggests its use as an arrow poison. The popular name Wolfsbane is believed to relate to ancient times when *Aconitum* served as a wolf poison. Its toxicity results from several monobasic alkaloids, including aconine and aconitine. Symptoms, which occur within a few hours of ingestion, include tingling and numbness of the tongue and mouth, a sensation of ants crawling over the body, nausea and vomiting, labored breathing, cold and clammy skin, and giddiness. More powerful than prussic acid, a dose of one to six and a half milligrams causes fatality in an adult.

A fourteen-year-old boy ate leaves of *A. napellus* (Common Monkshood) and was dead two hours later. A man mistook the root of *A. napellus* for horseradish, and a small portion on the tip of his knife killed him within a few hours. In 1841, a disgruntled Irish housewife sprinkled *A. napellus* over her husband's greens; he died three hours later.[8] Many poisons will be surveyed in the succeeding chapters; however, the discussion of *Datura, Cicuta, Veratrum,* and *Aconitum* has established that plant poisons can impair body functions, cause excruciating pain for weeks at less-than-lethal doses, or kill quickly and horribly. Particularly in the case of *Cicuta* and *Aconitum,* extremely small doses can lead to fatality. Further, plant poisons can kill in a number of ways: they depress respiration to the point of death, they paralyze the heart muscle, and they bring about coma and convulsions. Finally, toxic chemical agents carried in poisonous plants tend to be alkaloids, acids, resins, and glycosides, occurring singly or in combinations.

About five hundred years ago, Theophrastus Paracelso (sometimes identified as Paracelsus), a Swiss biologist who claimed that everything he knew came from a witch, left this axiom: "Dosis sola facit venenum" ("The dose alone makes a poison"). Most North American Indian poisons were also taken medicinally for a variety of ailments. The knowledge of dosage, as well as the general effects of the substance, made the difference between a potion of life and one of death.

Chapter 2

Nonmilitary Poisons

Whereas only specialists possessed knowledge of a wide variety of poisons, most North American Indians were well versed on the subject of suicidal agents as well as compounds for fishing, hunting, and protection from pests. Although researchers found gathering information about poisons generally difficult, informants were more forthcoming about those used in the food quest and for suicide, which usually stemmed from a broken heart.

Growing throughout Native North America, the white, fleshy root of genus *Cicuta* stands out as the suicide plant. In the Northeast Culture Area, the "suicide root" (*Cicuta masculata*—Spotted Water Hemlock) was first mentioned by Father Sagard, who worked among the Huron in 1632.[1] Long-time enemies of the Huron, the Iroquois (a confederation of the Seneca, Mohawk, Cayuga, Oneida, and Onondaga) are often noted for taking their own lives with *C. masculata*. Although most Indian informants pointed out that once a victim ingested the root, he or she could not be resuscitated, an Iroquois informant claimed that if a finely chopped muskrat skin with the hair attached was quickly administered, a chance for survival existed.[2] An Iroquois colleague warned the researcher that the "suicide root" was so dangerous that if one did not wash his or her hands thoroughly after handling it, convulsions would result.[3]

The suicide root was used by the Delaware and common among Central Algonquians.[4] In the Southeast Culture Area, *C. masculata* is mentioned in connection with the Tutelo,[5] as well as the Cherokee, who thought that small doses consumed over four consecutive days would result in sterility. Elders would chew small portions to divine the time of their death, believing that imminent demise would follow disorientation and a lack of dizziness would auger for long life.[6]

In the northern Plains Culture Area, the Blackfoot (a confederacy of the Kainah, Piegan, and Siksika) chose *C. occidentalis* root (Western

Water Hemlock) for suicide.[7] *C. virosa* (Long-Leafed Water Hemlock, Cowbane, Mackenzie's Water Hemlock) was preferred by a number of tribes in the subarctic forests,[8] and in the Northwest Coast Culture Area, the Kwakiutl selected *C. douglasii* (Douglas's Water Hemlock). The Inuit (Eskimo), including those of the Kuskokwim River region and Ninvak Island, and tribes in Alaska favored *C. virosa*.[9]

Although *Cicuta* was the preeminent suicide agent, except in arid regions where it was seldom found, a number of other poison plants— *Datura wrightii* (Sacred Thornapple), for example—were reported for the White Mountain Apache; the Western Keres of the Southwest Culture Area; and the Mahuna, Coahuila, and Diegueno of California. In his benchmark work on North American Indian ethnobotany, Daniel Moerman lists the Southern Carrier, Bella Coola, Blackfoot, Haisla and Hanaksiala, Okonagan-Colville, Oweekeno, Salish, Shuswap, Blackfoot, Cherokee, Cowlitz, and Thompson as utilizing *Veratrum viride* (American False Hellebore).[10] In addition to *C. masculata,* the Iroquois chose *Angelica venenosa* (Hairy Angelica) and *A. atropurpureas* (Purplestem Angelica). The Clallam, Lakota, Snohomish, and Klamath used *Conium masculatum* (Poison Hemlock).

North American Indians turned their knowledge of poisons to the animal world to aid in the food quest, most commonly fishing. Southeastern Indians caught fish by the following method:

[They] ... gather horse chestnuts and different sorts of roots, which having pounded pretty fine, and steeped a while in a trough, they scatter this mixture over the surface of a middle-sized pond, and stir it about with poles till the water is sufficiently impregnated with the intoxicating bittern. The fish are soon inebriated and make to the surface of the water, with their bellies uppermost. It seems that fish catched [*sic*] in this manner are not poisoned, but only stupefied for they prove very wholesome food to us who frequently use them. When they are in good water, they revive in a few minutes.[11]

The fish toxins of the Southeastern Indians momentarily stupefied, but did not kill, the fish. Most fish poisons of North American tribes impaired fish either by absorbing oxygen from the water, thus forcing them to the surface, or attacking the nervous system. The following passage describes the chemical fishing method of a California tribe:

After the last June freshet, when the river was running very low, all
of the inhabitants of a village or of several neighboring rancherias
would assemble together at some convenient place on the river.
The squaws were each provided with a quantity of the flesh bulbs,
which they deposed in a common heap and proceeded to mash up
on the rocks. A weir 6 to 7 feet high had in the meantime been
constructed by the men by driving willow sticks into the riverbed
and then lashing them together by means of redbud bark. Bushel
after bushel of the crushed pulp was thrown into the water and
thoroughly stirred in. Much of the finer material passed through
the weir, the large pieces were again taken out and again crushed
and thrown into the water. The Indians, stationed all along the
stream for 3 miles or so, added fresh bulbs here and there and kept
the water in a state of thorough agitation. After a very short time
all of the fish, and also the eels, but not the frogs, were so stupefied
by the poison that they floated to the surface and were quickly cap-
tured, either by hand or by the use of a shallow, coarse-meshed
basket.[12]

In California, *Croton setigerus* (Turkey Mullen) was sometimes mixed
with *Chlorogalum pomeridianum* (Soaproot) to poison fish in the Mendocino County area.[13] The Indian removed the *C. setigerus* from the water
after a sufficient take of fish and piled it on the bank to dry for later use.[14]

The methods of "poisoning" fish described above were found
throughout the country; however, as with the Southeastern and California examples, minor variations accommodated water conditions.
Weirs were constructed if the current flowed briskly; however, they
were not needed in natural ponds or areas where slight whirlpool effects
in the current contained the poisonous plants in one locality.

Although only a few plants were known for suicide, the Indians of
California and elsewhere were aware of dozens to stun or kill fish. In
South America, for example, more than a hundred species were docu-
mented as "fish poisons."[15] The Yuki and Konkow mashed *Aesculus cal-
ifornica* (California Buckeye), and the Konkow applied this method for
Trichostema lanceolatum (Vinegar Weed; camphor weed), as did the Num-
laki.[16] The Klamath used *T. lanceolatum, Eremocarpus setigerus* (Dove
Weed), and *C. pomeridianum* (Soaproot);[17] the Kawaiisu *Smilacina stel-*

lata (False Solomon's Seal).[18] California tribes such as the Cahuilla, Costanoan, Mahuma, and Mendocino utilized *Croton californicus* (Croton); and *C. pomeridianum* was found in the arsenal of the Costanoan, Cahuilla, Pomo, Yuki, Miwok, and Mendocino, who also included *Marah oreganos* (Oregon Bigroot). The Kashaya Pomo preferred *M. fabaceus* (Common Manroot) not only for local rivers, but also for tidal pools.[19] Various California tribes found *Cocculus indicus* (Fish Berry) to be effective.

In the Columbia-Frazer Plateau Culture Area, the Okanagan-Colville mixed about ten tops and roots of *Lomatium dissectum* (Chocolate Tips) in a bucket of water and emptied the contents into a creek. The fish taken in this fashion were safe to eat if gathered immediately.[20] In the Great Basin Area, the Paiutes fished with *E. setigerus*.[21]

The Southeast Culture Area presents many examples of fish poisons. The Cherokee chose among pounded walnut bark, western buckeye (*Aesculus*),[22] various species of *Tephrosia* (Goat's Rue),[23] *Polygonum hydropiper* (Knotweed),[24] and *Yucca filamentosa* (Bear Grass).[25]

North of the Cherokee, the Delaware and Algonquian powdered the nuts of *Aesculus glabra* (Chestnut) to deposit in a stream. The chemicals stupefied the fish, leading some Indian informants to refer to the powder jokingly as "fish peyote."[26]

A Choctaw authority wrote, "Three stupefacients—coral berries, parts of the less potent buckeye plant, and the devil's shoestring—were thrown into still water to stun fish, which could then be gathered easily from the surface."[27]

The North American Indians possessed poisons not only for fish, but also for the smallest insects to the largest mammals. The Cherokee found that mandrake worked as an insecticide,[28] and they smeared mashed Goldenseal root mixed with bear fat on their bodies as a repellent.[29] The Cree repelled fleas and gnats with Canada Fleabane.[30] The Makah of the northwest coast removed lice with powdered hemlock bark, the Castanoan of California with *Eschscholzia californica* (California Poppy), and the Seri of Baja, California, with a shampoo of the crushed fruits of *Matelea pringlei* (Milkvine) boiled in water. They then combed the powdered leaves of *Simmondsia chinensis* (Jojoba) into their hair.[31]

A variety of pests besides insects were targeted. The Okanagan-Colville treated coyote bait with *Ranunculus glaberrimus* (Sagebrush

Buttercup). The Cherokee poisoned wolves with *Calycanthus floridus* (Carolina Allspice) and rats with *Chimaphila masculata* (Spotted Wintergreen).[32] Wolf poison was sometimes needed to protect new graves.

Some of the largest animals on the planet fell victim to Native American poisons. The native peoples of the Aleutians, as well as those of Kodiak Island, dipped their harpoons in aconite to kill whales.[33] Only a single thrust was required. An explorer of the Northwest Coast in the late 1700s wrote of the Kodiak Island people,

> They also add poison to their arrows, and the Aconite is the drug adopted for this purpose. Selecting the roots of such plants as grow alone, these roots are dried and pounded, or grated; water is then poured upon them, and they are kept in a warm place till fermented; when in this state, the men anoint the points of their arrows, or lances, which makes the wound that may be inflicted mortal.[34]

The Yurok, Tolowa, and Karok of northwestern California rubbed a juice processed from *Toxicodendron diversilobum* (Pacific Poison Oak) on their arrows to hunt big game.[35] The Okanagan-Colville Indians mashed *Juniperus scopulorum* (Rocky Mountain Juniper) berries in water and soaked their arrowheads. They said that when a deer was hit, its blood would thicken unnaturally and slow the animal as it attempted escape. This poison did not affect the edibility of the meat. The Thompson Indians, neighbors of the Okanagan-Colville, painted the sap of *Cornus sericea* (Red Osier Dogwood) on their hunting arrows.[36] Many Indians of the Canadian forests referred to *C. masculata* as "beaver poison" because of its common use in beaver hunting. The effects of hunting poisons on animals ranged from an irritating sting to impaired coordination to death. Many of these same plants were also used in warfare.

Indian knowledge of poisons was impressive and, according to early witnesses, widely applied; however, a great fear of them existed among California tribes. "The Indians profess to be in great and perpetual dread of being poisoned by one another, and no one will taste anything handed to him by one who is not a member of his family, unless the other tastes it first."[37]

An observer of North Carolina Indians, John Brickell, wrote in 1731,

"The Indians are so well acquainted with the poisons that this country produces that they have been known to poison whole families, and most parts of the town; and it is certain, that they can poison a running spring or fountain of water, that whoever drinks therefore will soon after infallibly die."[38] Another early commentator on North Carolina Indians wrote of "the art they have, and often practice of poisoning one another; which is done by a large white spongy root that grows in the fresh marshes, which is one of their poisons, not but that they have many other drugs which they poison one another withal."[39] John Swanton, a noted ethnologist, said of the Algonquian culture that the "destruction of those who were disliked by poisoning was fairly common."[40]

Many groups in the Northeast Culture Area had knowledge of poisons. The Abnaki recognized the toxic qualities of *Caltha palustris* (Marsh Marigold) and *Aconitum delphinifolium* (Larkspur Leaf Monkshood). The Mohegan considered *Aralia spinosa* (Devil's Walking Stick) and *Podophyllum peltatum* (Mayapple or American Mandrake) poisonous; and the Mohegan, Penobscot, and Meskawki knew of *Arisaema triphyllum* (Jack in the Pulpit). All the tribes of New England were aware of the poisonous properties of *A. triphyllum*.[41]

The Cree were cognizant of the dangers of *Aconitum heterophyllum* (Atis), *Kalmia latifolia* (Mountain Laurel), and *Caltha palustris*.[42] The Chippewa (also known as the Ojibwe, or Ojibwa) were wary of *Toxicodendron vernix* (Poison Ivy) and *Pastinaca sativa* (Wild Parsnip), as were the Potawatomi. Both plants cause dermatitis (inflammation of the skin).

Of the Northeastern tribes, the Iroquois are the most widely documented on all aspects of their culture, including poisons. They mixed the leaves and roots of *Lycopus virginicus* (Virginia Horehound), *Cardamines bulbosa* (Spring Cress), *Trillium ovatum* (Toadstool), or *A. venenosa* with food as a murder weapon.[43] They scraped the dried root of *Dipsacus aylventris* (Common Teasel) and *Celastrus scandens* (American Bittersweet) into a powder, a pinch of which in a victim's coffee or tea would kill within two days. Iroquois informants reported that evil people who were jealous of another's baby would dip a finger in a liquid version of this poison and touch it to the baby's lips.[44]

To contaminate an enemy's liquor or water canteen, the poisoner would add pieces of *Anemone canadensis* (Meadow Anemone) root.[45] The Iroquois included *Cardamine rhomboidea* (Bulbous Bittercress), the berries of *C. scandens*, *Eupatorium perfoliatum* (Boneset or Feverwort), *L. asper*

(Rough Bugleweed), *D. stramonium* (Jimson Weed), *L. virginicus, Onopordum acanthium* (Scotch Cottonthistle), *Parthenocissus quinquefolia* (Virginia Creeper), *P. peltatum, Sisyrinchium montanum* (Mountain Blue-eyed Grass), and *Veronicastrum virginicum* (Culver's Root) in poison making.[46]

The Algonquin recognized the toxicity of *C. palustris* and *Kalmia angustifolia* (Sheep Laurel). All of those questioned knew of the latter and cautioned against confusing it with *Ledum groenlandicumds* (Labrador Tea).[47]

The Menomini concocted poison from the berries of *Nemopanthus mucronata* (Mountain Holly), the root of *Sambucus canadensis* (American Elder),[48] and the leaves of *Comptonia peregrina* (Sweet Fern). The Ojibwe used the root of *Pastinaca sativa* (Wild Parsnip).[49]

The Mohegan and the Penobscot poisoned with the finely chopped root of *A. triphyllum* and the berries and roots of *Phytolacca americana* (American Pokeweed).[50]

The Ojibwe and Potawatomi used *P. sativa* as a toxin. The Chippewa claimed that *Dirca palustris* (Leatherwood) berries were narcotic and poisonous.[51]

The Micmac, Arctic Inuit, and Thompson Indians knew *Actaea rubra* (Red Baneberry) to be toxic. The Micmac, too, were aware of the poisonous qualities of *K. ˙angustifolia,* as were the Montagnais.

In the Southeast Culture Area, the Creek Indians of Georgia and Alabama learned that the root of *Lomatium nuttalli* (Nuttall's Biscuitroot) was poisonous if eaten in the winter. The Cherokee discovered *C. douglasii, P. americana, Oplopanax horridus* (Devil's Club), *Osmorhiza berteroi* (Sweet Cicely), *V. viride,* and the root joints of *P. peltatum.*

The Rappahannock in Virginia found *D. stramonium* and *Solanum nigrum* (Black Nightshade) to be dangerous,[52] and the Catawba in South Carolina concocted poison from both *Chenopodium ambrosioides* (Jerusalem Oak) and *D. stramonium.*[53]

On the plains, the Blackfeet of Montana understood the toxicity of *Veratrum californicum, C. douglasii, O. horridus, O. berteroi,* and *V. viride.* East of the Blackfeet, the Lakota Sioux poisoned with *Conium masculatus* (Poison Hemlock), *Disporum hookeri* (Drops of Gold), *Nymphaea ordorata* (American White Pond Lily), *Symphoricarpos albus* (Snowberry), *Triteleia grandiflora* (Wild Hyacinth), *V. viride,* and *Zigadenus venenosus* (Meadow Death Camas).[54] The Oglala Sioux applied the poisonous qualities of the root of *C. scandens.*[55]

On the central Plains, the Pawnee, who hunted along the Platte and Republican Rivers, experienced the dangers of *Dichrophyllum marginatum* (Snow on the Mountain).[56] South of the Pawnee, the Ponca found *Toxicodendron pubescens* (Poison Oak) to be a major skin irritant. The Cheyenne, who lived west of the Ponca and Pawnee, attacked their enemies magically with *Pentaphylloides floribunda* (Shrubby Cinquefoil) and *Pulsatilla patens* (Eastern Pasque Flower).[57]

The Kutenai, who roamed the fringes of the Rocky Mountains, considered *C. douglasii* to be very poisonous, and to their south the Flathead made poison from *Frangula purshiana* (Pursh's Buckthorn). The Indians near San Antonio, Texas, found the scarlet bean of *Broussonetia secundiflora* to be so lethal that ingesting one bean would kill a man.[58]

West of the Rocky Mountains, in the area known as the Great Basin, the Paiutes of Oregon saw that horses poisoned by *Z. venenosus* root foamed at the mouth and humans experienced chills and convulsions before dying.[59] The Paiute also viewed *N. ordorata, S. albus, T. grandiflora,* and *V. viride* as harmful.[60]

The Ute of western Colorado used the toxic properties of *Fritillaria atropurpurea* (Spotted Missionsbells) and *Zigadenus nuttalli.* The Gosiute of the Great Basin treated *Aconitum fischeri* (Fisher's Monkshood), *Brickellia grandiflora* (Tassel Flower), and *Delphinium bicolor* (Low Larkspur) as poisons.[61]

The Cowlitz of western Washington considered *O. horridus* and *V. viride* toxic. To their north in southern British Columbia, the Okanagan-Colville understood the poisonous nature of *V. viride, C. douglasii, O. horridus, O. berteroi, N. ordorata, S. albus, T. grandiflora, Coprinus comatus* (Inkycap Mushroom), *Z. venenosus, Aconitum columbianum* (Columbian Monkshood), *L. dissectum,* and *Lonicera involucrata* (Twinberry Biscuit).[62] The Okanagan-Colville knew that the berries of *J. scopulorum* and *Platanthera dilatata* (White Bog-Orchid) were poisonous.[63] In fact, *V. viride* was the most poisonous plant in the Okanagan-Colville territory.

The Thompson Indians, neighbors to the Okanagan-Colville, used the toxic qualities of *V. viride, O. berteroi, O. horridus, Cicuta spp., L. involucrate, A. columbianum, L. dissectum, A. rubra, Lipinus polyhyllus* (Bigleaf Lupine), *R. glaberrimus, Ranunculus repens* (Creeping Buttercup), *R. sceleratus* (Celeryleaf Buttercup), *Zigadenus elegans, V. californicum,* and *L. involucrate.*[64] They believed that one or two berries of *S. albus* were lethal for humans. As for *Artemisia dracunculus* (Wormwood), the Thompson Indians discovered that it was lethal only if it entered the bloodstream.

North of the Thompson Indians, the Shuswap identified eight plant species as poisonous to men and animals: *C. douglasii, Galium boreale* (Northern Bedstraw), *P. dilatata, Sium suave* (Hemlock Water Parsnip), *V. viride, Z. venenosus, N. ordorata, S. albus,* and *T. grandiflora.*[65]

In California, the Mendocino used *Asclepias fascicularis* (Mexican Whorled Milkweed) flowers, several species of *Cicuta,* and the thorns of *Crataegus rivularis* (River Hawthorn). *Phoradendron leucarpum* (Oak Mistletoe) and *Quercus chrysolepis* (Canyon Live Oak) nut were also in their repertoire of poisons, as were *S. nigrum, V. viride, Z. venenosus, T. grandiflora, Heracleum maximum* (common Cow Parsnip), *Mahonia aquifolium* (Hollyleaved Barberry or Oregon Grape), *M. oreganos, S. albus, Datura stramonium,* and *N. ordorata.*[66]

In northern California and vicinity, the Karok used *H. maximum, Mahonia aquifolium, M. oreganos,* and *S. nigruma* as poisons; their neighbors to the west, the Yurok, *T. diversilobum.* The Klamath, on the northeast edge of the California Culture Area, identified *C. masculata* as lethal.[67]

On the coast of northern California, the Pomo included *N. ordorata, S. albus, T. grandiflora, V. viride, Z. venenosus, Clintonia andrewsiana* (Western Bluebead Lily), *Amanita muscaria* (Gill Fungi), and various species of *Trillium* in their poison taxonomy.[68]

The Yuki, on the northern borders of the Pomo, knew *N. ordorata, S. albus, T. grandiflora, V. viride, Z. venenosus,* and *Anthemis cotula* (Stinking Chamomile) as poisons. On the northern edge of the California Area, the Tolowa understood the toxic properties of *L. involucrate, A. columbianum, C. douglasii,* and *L. dissectum;* and still farther north, the Quinault recognized those of *V. viride, Symphoricarpos albus,* and *L. -dissectum.*[69]

In southern California, the Cahuilla and Diequeno groups used *Cryptantha crassisepala* (Thick Sepal Catseye), *D. stramonium,* and *Zigadenus elgans.* The Cahuilla were aware of *Asclepias subulata* (Rush Milkweed), *Chamaesyce polycarpa* (Small Seed Sandmat), *Ricinus communis* (castor bean), and *Sucucta spp.* (dooder). Chumash sorcerers favored *Zigadenus fremontii* for killing.[70]

In the Southwest Culture Area, the Indians around Mesa Verde knew *Delphinium nelsonii* (Crowfoot), *Zigadenus spp.,* and *Physalis fend-*

leri (Ground Cherry) to have poisonous qualities. The Navaho poisoned with *Hackelia floribunda* (Many-Flowered Stickweed) and *Urtica gracilis* and believed that *Hordeum jubatum* (Wild Barley) was so lethal that a man would die from it merely being inside his mouth.[71] The Navaho called *Astragalus spp.* (Milkvetch) *Te'il' aganiih*, "the deadly plant," and referred to an unidentified species of *Leguminosae* as "plant which is bad for the mind" because its victim became "crazy" before dying.[72] The Navaho also found *Echinocereus coccineus* (Scarlet Hedgehog Cactus), *Vicia faba* (Horse Bean), *Sonchus asper* (Spiny Sowthistle), *H. floribunda*, and *Hordeum juatum* (Foxtail Barley) to have poisonous qualities.

The White Mountain Apache and such Pueblo groups as the Acoma, Laguna, Cochita, and Zia, applied *C. crassisepala, D. wrightii*, and *Z. elegans* as poisons.[73]

In the Northwest Coast Culture Area, most Salish groups knew of *V. viride, C. douglasii, O. horridus*, and *O. berteroi*.[74] The Bella Coola of British Columbia believed the inner core of *V. viride* and *V. eschscholtzii* to be the most lethal section of the plants and that death would ensue from holding a piece in the mouth even if it were not swallowed. They also considered *Physocarpus capitatus* (Pacific Ninebark), *Streptopus amplexifolius* (Wild Cucumber), *L. dissectum*, and *S. albus* to be dangerous.[75]

The Haisla of the west coast of British Columbia identified *C. douglassi, O. horridus, L. dissectum, S. albus, O. berteroi, V. viride*, and *Oenanthe sarmentosa* (Water Parsley) as poisonous. The Oweekeno, Kitasoo, and the northern Wakashan and Tsimshian speakers used *V. viride, Z. venenosus, C. douglasii*, and *O. sarmentosa*.[76]

Many times legitimate medicines were delivered as an overdose, and the potency of chemicals was enhanced in the minds of those involved by belief in what we would call the putative magical qualities of the plant. The versatility of *V. viride* as explored by various tribes of the west coast of British Columbia is seen in the following description:

> This highly toxic plant has been widely used for medicinal and ritual applications by the native groups of the Pacific Northwest. The Haisla used it in poultices, in infusions to be taken internally with great caution, to produce snuff used for colds and as an emetic which, if taken in excess, can be extremely dangerous and even fatal. When present, this plant is believed to repel ghosts, illness, and evil.[77]

The Oweekeno found *Epilobium angustifolium* (Fireweed), *Ribes lacustre* (Prickly Current), and the berries of *O. horridus* to have noxious qualities. As with most Northwest Coast groups, they considered *C. douglasii, O. berteroi, L. dissectum, S. albus,* and *V. viride* to be dangerous.[78]

The Kwakiutl, who inhabited the northeastern part of Vancouver Island and the adjacent islands and mainland to the east, were knowledgeable of *C. douglasii, O. horridus, O. berteroi, V. viride, A. columbianum, L. dissectum, L. involucrate, S. albus,* and *O. sarmentosa.*

In the southern sector of the Northwest Coast Culture Area, the Makah knew of *A. columbianum, C. douglasii, L. dissectum,* and the berries of *L. involucrate.* In the area of Puget Sound, the Snohomish recognized *E. angustifolium, R. lacustre, C. masculatus,* and *D. hookeri* while their neighbors, the Skagit, used *Trillium.* The Clallam applied *C. masculatus* and *D. hookeri* as poisons.[79]

Among most tribes of Alaska (Koyukon, Tanana, Kutchin, Han, Nabesna, Tannaina, Ingalik, Athtena), the poisonous qualities of *A. delphinifolium, C. palustris, Iris setosa* (Beachhead Iris or Blue Flag), *Ledum palustre* (Marsh Tea or Wild Rosemary), *Lupinus arcticus* (Arctic Lupine), *Ranunculus pallasii* (Pallas's Buttercup), *Hedysarum boreale* (Mackensie's Sweet Vetch), *C. douglasii, O. horridus, O. berteroi,* and *V. viride* were recognized.[80]

To the list of Alaskan poisons should be added *Z. elegans, C. mackensiana* (Poison Water Hemlock), *A. rubra,* and *Astragalus oxytropis.* *Zigadenus* contains the toxic alkaloid zigadenine throughout the plant. Symptoms of poisoning include excess salivation, nausea, vomiting, lowered temperature, weakness with staggering, prostration, and difficulty breathing. As few as six berries of the Baneberry plant can elicit painful burning in the stomach, increased pulse, and dizziness.[81] Some members of the family have the ability to absorb from the soil such minerals as selenium and molybdenum, which even in small quantities produce extremely toxic symptoms.[82]

The Carrier Indians, who ranged on the southern edges of the Subarctic Culture Area, knew of the poisonous qualities of *V. viride, S. albus,* and *L. dissectum.*

Native Americans of the far north had knowledge of a variety of plant poisons. *Equisetum spp.* was a "magical poison" for hated guests of the Aleuts. The flowers of *Ranunculus occidentalis* (Western Buttercup) would cause a person to "waste away to nothing."[83] Another powerful plant of

the Aleutian peoples, as well as neighboring Inuit and Indian populations, was *Aconitum spp.*, which often poisoned whaling harpoons and
arrows. The Inupiat counted *Aconitum delphinifolium*, *Caltha palustris*,
Hedysarum boreale (Plains Sweet Broom), *Iris setosa*, *Ledum palustre* (Wild
Rosemary), *Lupinus arcticus* (Arctic Lupine), and *Ranunculus pallasii* (Pallas's Buttercup) in their poison inventory. The Kuskokwagmiut recognized the dangerous qualities of *Cicuta virosa*.[84]

North American Indians expended a greater variety of poisons
against insect pests than game animals, fish, and humans. They created
poisons to kill and others to repel. Repellents were applied to the body,
burned as smudges, or sprinkled on clothing. Every culture area accumulated a broad repertoire of insecticides.

A compound made from *Thalictrum occidentale* (Western Meadow
Rue) served the Blackfoot as an insecticide. They prepared a repellent
from the dried flowers of *Matricaria matricaiodes* (Pineapple Weed) and
applied an oil from crushed juniper berries to the skin.[85] The Piikani
(also known as the Peigan), a member of the Blackfoot Confederacy,
rubbed the juice from *Artemisia frigida* (Woman Sage) on their bodies to
repel mosquitoes.[86] The Osage protected their potato crop from insects
with a decoction based around *Juniperus spp.* (Cedar or Juniper).[87] The
Lakota fought mosquitoes with a smudge of the leaves of *Psoralea
tenuifloia* (Few-Flowered Psoralea).[88]

Claiming that the solution would kill the potato bugs in the ground,
as well as the bugs themselves, the Menomini sprinkled a tea from
P. peltatum on infested potato plants.[89]

The Cree crushed *Gymnocarpium dryopteris* (Oak Fern) leaves both to
repel mosquitoes and treat bites[90] and used a smudge of Canada fleabane
against fleas and gnats.[91] They also burned the fruiting bodies of *Fomes
fomentarius* (Tinder Fungus) to repel mosquitoes and flies.[92]

As a mosquito repellent, the Iroquois preferred *Corylus cornuta*
(Beaked Hazel) either alone or mixed with bear fat while the Chipewyan burned spruce boughs (*Picea mariana*, Blackspruce) outside their
homes.[93]

The Rappahannock repelled fleas with *Hedeoma pulegioides* (American
Pennyroyal),[94] and the Tuscarora simply smeared bear grease over their
bodies.[95] The "bear grease" or "bear fat" often described in association
with insect repellents in the Southeast was actually a refined and scented
body oil rendered from bear fat.

The Cherokee mixed a tea of *Hydrangea arborscens* (Sevenbark) with bear grease,[96] soaked corn seed in one made from *Viola rotundifolia* root[97] (Round-Leaved Violet), or brewed tea from the root of *C. masculata*.[98] They protected corn seeds from infestation by soaking them in the mashed root of *P. peltatum*.[99]

The Cherokee pounded the large rootstock of *Hydrastis canadensis* (Goldenseal) with bear fat and smeared it on their bodies when insects were bothersome.[100] They fought flies and poisoned crows that threatened their gardens with the root of *Amianthium muscaetoxicum* (Fly Poison or Stagger Grass).[101]

The Indians of Mendocino County, California, crushed California Laurel (*Ubellularia californica*) leaves and spread them about their lodgings to repel fleas. To drive off flying pests, they created a smudge of the powdered leaves of *Croton texennsis* (Texas Croton).[102]

Some tribes in southern California rubbed *Allium spp.* (Wild Onion) on their bodies,[103] and others applied *Pogogyne parviflora* (Wild Petunia).[104] The Maidu added water to the pulverized seeds of *Aquilegia formosa* (Columbine) and rid themselves of head lice with the paste.[105] In fact, they possessed several methods of delousing. They rubbed the dried and pulverized roots of *Delphinium spp.* (Larkspur) mixed with water on their heads[106] and also decocted *Equisetum spp.* (Horsetail), which worked against lice and fleas.[107] They concocted a tea from *L. glandulosum* to kill fleas and another from *Orobanche spp.* (Broom Rape) to kill lice. Both were applied as a skin wash.

The Costanoan rubbed a decoction of *Eschscholzia spp.* (California Poppy) into their hair to treat lice[108] and rid their houses of fleas with a smudge of *U. californica*.[109] The Kawaiisu used *Osmorhiza spp.* as a general insecticide[110] and burned California bay leaves in their houses as a flea repellent.[111]

The Owens Valley Paiute infused *Sphenosciadium capitellatus* (Rander's Button) root to repel lice.[112] Among the Yurok of California Bay, leaves of *U. californica* were scattered among stored acorns to prevent insect infestation.

The Chumash protected themselves from fleas with *Heterotheca grandiflorida* (Telegraph Weed),[113] and the Haida of the Queen Charlotte Islands killed lice with *O. horridus*.[114] The Dena'ina of interior Alaska possessed a number of insect poisons. A smudge of *Gramineae spp.* (Sedge) repelled, and a tea of the boiled root of *Delphinium glaucum* (Larkspur) became a body wash against lice and fleas. *Achillea borealis* (Yarrow) and

Artemisia absinthium (Wormwood or Absinth) were rubbed on the skin and clothing to repel mosquitoes.[115]

The wide variety of nonmilitary poisons of the North American Indians is impressive. Applications of poison warfare other than arrow poisoning, its most typical use, will be discussed below. First, however, a survey of poison-arrow usage around the world, with an emphasis on military application, must be addressed to better evaluate North American Indian biochemical warfare, particularly that of arrow poisons. Without such a preliminary survey, there would be no way to establish a comparative context or understand where Native Americans stand in terms of premodern chemical warfare. Was their application of chemical warfare typical or unusual? Was the number of arrow poisons in their martial repertoire large, normal, or relatively small?

Chapter 3

World Survey of Arrow Poisoning

E ven a brief survey of the relevant literature reveals that, from ancient to modern times, poisoned arrows have been employed in
almost all parts of the world. As for the dawn of arrow poisoning,
there lies only conjecture. Perhaps ancient humans first encountered the
possibilities when they noticed more serious wounds and infections resulting from weapons coated with the dried remains of their prey's blood
and gore.

The Bible records the cries of Job: "The arrows of the Almighty
pierce men, and my spirit drinks their poison." Homer mentions in
the *Odyssey* that Ulysses had knowledge of poisoning arrows and that
Achilles was killed by an arrow wound in his heel.[1] One may ask how
such a wound could have been fatal unless the arrow was poisoned.

For killing his wife and children, Hercules, son of Zeus, was confronted with the punishment of the Twelve Labors. After completing his
second task, killing the Hydra that lived in the swamp of Lerna, he
dipped his arrows in her blood to poison them. The myth continues that
in his fourth labor, he killed the great boar of Mount Erymanthus with
poisoned arrows, and in his sixth, a flock of man-eating birds with
bronze beaks and claws.

The most widespread method of poisoning arrows among North
American Indians mirrors that of the ancient Greeks, who buried the remains of deadly adders until putrefied. The finished product contained
not only snake venom, but also gangrene and tetanus bacteria.[2] In the
fourth century, Quintillian, lieutenant of the Roman general Maximus,
confronted the Franks, who fired large poisoned arrows from catapults
behind a thick log palisade. Gregory de Tours wrote that wounds
inflicted by these Frankish arrows would surely cause death.[3] The Romans employed the Numidians, whom they first encountered during
the Punic Wars, as mercenaries because their poisoned arrows terrorized
the Teutonic tribes.[4]

Aristotle, Strabo, and Pliny wrote that the Celts and Gauls poisoned their arrows with the juice of *Lineum,* a genus related to hellebore. The Celts applied sap from the Yew tree, and the Dalmatians and Daces, *Aster helenium* (Sneezeweed).[5] The Gauls used aconite, the favored arrow poison in both Europe and Asia, with fifty species known in Europe and twenty-four in India.

The Scythians, Aristotle reported, poisoned their arrows with a mixture of snake venom and putrefied blood. Classical literature is replete with references to arrow poisoning by the peoples of the Black Sea and Asia Minor.[6]

A 1644 English book on "field sports" offers the following description of preparing an arrow poison known as the crossbowman's herb:

This decoction is made of the roots of the white Hellebore, which should be gathered towards the end of August as it is then at its best season and strength. The way to treat them is to take off all earth and any kind of viscous matter which may adhere to them and wash them well. After this they should be pounded and placed under a press to extract all their juice, which will have to be carefully strained and then put over a fire to boil. All froth and viscosity which may remain must be skimmed off the juice. When this is done, the juice must be strained again and then set in the sun from ten o'clock in the morning till the day declines. This process will have to be repeated for three or four days or more. Each day before the juice is set in the sun it must be strained, when it should be like syrup, and of the same color but thicker. If you put a straw or a bit of stick in it, it should adhere to it, and that which gathers together most quickly and which if smelt makes people sneeze violently, is the strongest.[7]

The long history of arrow poisoning in Asia reaches into relatively modern times. Customary behaviors surrounding the concoction of arrow poison among the Ainu of Hokkaido indicate that the pattern precedes the rise of historical Japanese civilization. In the late nineteenth century, Europeans often accompanied the Ainu on hunts and described their observations, including those on arrow poisons.[8] The Ainu prepared such deadly poisons that a bear would die in a matter of hours after being struck.

Ainu arrow poison was based around two species of *Aconitum: A. ferox* (Indian Aconite) and *A. japonicum* (Japanese Aconite), two of the most lethal members of the genus. In the spring the Ainu dug, peeled, and dried the roots in the sun, after which they pounded them into a powder between two stones.[9] They then added the gall bladders of three foxes[10] and boiled the mixture in a quart of water until it was reduced by half. After straining the concoction, they allowed it to dry to a pulpy consistency. At this point, the poison maker added six crushed poisonous spiders and more water and boiled it to a gummy consistency. Some Ainu poison makers would bury the compound for several days, but others applied the sticky mass directly to specially designed poison-carrying arrows.

Western observers witnessed that only a few Ainu men knew the secrets of poison and that they carried out their preparation with much secrecy and formality. To test the poison before applying it to arrows, one would touch a small piece to the tongue. If the poison was good, a numbing and tingling sensation would immediately occur in the mouth.

Their bamboo arrowhead was about two inches long and slightly excavated or channeled on one side. It was loosely affixed to a point shaft several inches in length, which was inserted into a reed shaft. The composite construction prevented a bear or man from removing the arrow because the head would disconnect within the victim's body.

The Ainu hunter dipped the arrowhead into pine-tree gum before applying a ball of poison the size of a pea in the channeled side, flattening it with his thumb. Finally, he once again dipped the arrowhead into the pine-tree gum, which kept the poison firmly attached.

None of the Ainu poison-arrow research mentions its use in combat. By the time Western observers had contacted the Ainu, the Japanese government had expressed strong disapproval of arrow poison and outlawed its manufacture.

North of the Ainu, the native peoples of Kamchatka-Kurile applied *Anemone virginiana* (Virginia Wind Flower) and *Anemone nemorosa* (Scarlet Wind Flower) to their arrows.[11]

Russian explorers in the Kurile Islands in the late 1700s reported the natives with a plant called Liutik. With a mixture made from the root, they painted their bodies and anointed their arrowheads to poison them.[12] The plant was later identified as a species of *Anemone*.

The first recorded Japanese encounter with enemies using poisoned arrows came in 1274 when Kublai Khan launched a force of 30,000 Koreans and Mongols in 450 ships against Japan at Hakata Bay on the island of Kyushu. The attackers excelled at massed cavalry maneuvering and armed themselves with javelins, maces, and poisoned arrows.[13]

The peoples of China are well known for their arrow poisons in both hunting and warfare.[14] *A. japonicum* was widely used in northern China. *The Book of Later Han* by Fan Ye (398–445) recounts an attack by the Xiongnu [Huns] against a town defended by the hero Geng Gong:

> Geng Gong climbed onto the ramparts, and led his soldiers into battle. He coated his arrows with a poison, and spread the rumor among the Xiongnu that the Han had sacred arrows, and the wounds of those who were hit would certainly be extraordinary. Then he used powerful crossbows to shoot these arrows. The barbarians who were hit noticed that their wounds were all frothing up. They were very frightened then.[15]

Many species of *Aconitum* flourished, especially in the mountainous regions of China, where hunters and warriors of Yunnan and Guangxi concocted arrow poisons into the twentieth century.[16] The Nosu of southwestern Szechwan devised a powerful arrow poison, as did the Miao of Kweichow and the peoples in southeastern China. In the Qing Dynasty, the Manchu rulers praised the skill of southwestern crossbowmen, who could shoot small birds on the fly with their poisoned arrows.[17] Chemical analysis determined that Miao poison was extracted from the root of *Aconitum spp.* and that of the Nosu from the leaves and stems and resembled the "black aconite" favored by some Tibetan groups.[18] The Burmese and Vietnamese also employed aconite arrow poison.[19] That of the Lhoba in southern Tibet had such toxicity that, while making it, they were compelled to cover their mouths and work with a following wind so that not even the smallest trace could blow into their eyes.

Francis Hamilton, a British medical doctor stationed on the Nepalese frontier in the early 1800s, dispatched an assistant into the mountains in search of plants that the local tribesmen used for poisoning arrows. The assistant returned with several species of *Ranunculus* (*Aconitum* is a member of the *Ranunculus* family), including *A. similax* (Greek derivation meaning "poisonous tree") and *A. trollius,* all known as *bish* by the mountain people. Referring to *Aconitum*, which he suspected as the key ingredient in the various *bish*, Hamilton wrote,

> This dreadful root, of which large quantities are annually imported, is equally fatal when taken into the stomach and when applied to wounds, and is in universal use throughout India for poisoning arrows; and there is too much reason to suspect for the worst of purposes. Its importation would indeed seem to require attention of the magistrate. The Gorkhalese [Goorkha] pretend that it is one of their principal securities against invasion from the low countries, and they could so infect all the water on the route by which an enemy was advancing as to occasion his certain destruction.[20]

The Goorkha and other tribes inhabiting the flanks of the Himalayas poisoned weapons with the root of *A. ferox*.[21] In an experiment to test the effectiveness of the poison, researchers injected two grains of the Goorkha's *bish* into the jugular of a "good-sized strong dog." The dog convulsed in one minute and was dead in three.[22]

The Abor of northeast India, neighbors of the Mishmis, live on the border between Assam and Tibet. Both groups use poison arrows that can kill tigers, buffaloes, and elephants in hunting and warfare. British medical doctor Sir Thomas R. Fraser, assigned to India in the mid-nineteenth century, wrote, "Our troops were assailed with poisoned arrows in Major-General Babbage's Abor Expedition of 1848, and they were used in most of the subsequent punitive expeditions, which also originated from the depredations of these turbulent tribesmen."[23]

In the last expedition against the Abor and Mishmis in 1911, the British "on many occasions were subjected to flights of poisoned arrows."[24] Medical officers treated six poison-arrow wounds, and three of the wounded died.

The Abor were forthcoming about the ingredients in their arrow poisons: *Aconitum* and *Croton* oil, pig's blood, serpent's venom, and the fruit and juice of several poisonous plants. Fraser's analysis identified *A. ferox* and sometimes *A. heterophyllum* (Atis).[25]

Fraser also studied *Entada scandens* (Sword Bean), another arrow poison ingredient, as well as Sri Lankan fish poison.[26] This plant, along with *Artocarpus integrifolia* (Jackwood) and *Feronia elephantum* (Elephant Apple), strengthened the lethal mix and lent an adhesive quality.

In comparing their arrow poisons, Fraser learned that *Croton* oil heavily influenced the Abor poison whereas *Aconitum* dominated that of the Mishmis. "From information derived from the tribesmen, arrows poisoned with croton are preferred in warfare, because, in their experience, death from aconite arrows can be generally prevented by merely washing the poison out of the wound with water; whereas *Croton* arrow wounds, even if so treated, cause local effects likely to result in death by secondary septic poisoning."[27]

The aconite-treated arrows of the Abor and Mishmis could kill an elephant (two and a half tons, or 2,540 kilograms) with thirteen arrows and a water buffalo (700 kilograms) with four or five. On the basis of the above figures, two arrows could kill a two-hundred-pound man. The most potent poison concoction Fraser examined was so deadly that one arrow could kill three men.[28]

Plants, particularly flowering ones, provided the poisons for North American Indian and Asian arrows; however, the Kung San (Bushmen) of the northern Khalahari Desert in southern Africa mixed one of their most effective arrow poisons from the larvae and pupae of *chrysomelid* beetles (*Diamphidia;* Arrow Poison Beetle). The cocoons live between twenty centimeters and one meter underground around the host plant, the dza tree (*Commiphora angolensis*). The grub of *Lebistina,* found near its host the marula tree, was also a source. *Lebistina,* fittingly, was the Roman goddess of corpses, funerals, and the underworld.

The Kung San simply squeezed the contents of the larvae/pupae on the arrow just behind the point, perhaps drying it over a fire, or they combined the contents of the *chrysomelid* beetle with crushed *Lebistina* and tree gum to augment the poison and create an adhesive. A third method entailed drying the larvae/pupae, grinding it to a powder, and reconstituting it with plant juice (adhesive) before applying it. The Kung San arrow poison could kill a rabbit-sized animal in only a few minutes, but they might have had to track large animals, such as giraffes, for days before the poison brought them down.

Bushmen in southwest Africa rub the extracted resin from the root of *Buphane toxicaria* (Oxbane) on a small stone, which they place in the mouth of a snake, usually the ringhals. They force venom out to mix with the resin and coat arrow and spear tips with the resulting gum.[29]

Longman and Walrond, archery historians, offer this comment about Bushmen arrow poisons:

The Bushmen use both vegetable and animal poisons. The former are chiefly obtained either from the bulb of the *Amaryllis toxicaria* [Upas Tree] or the juice of one of the *Euphorbias* [Milkwort]. Animal poisons are of several kinds, amongst them being the matter from the poison-gland of several kinds of snakes; they also, like the Ainu, use the juices from large black spiders. The most terrible poison of all, however, is made from the body of a grub called *N'gwa,* or *K'aa,* which drives any unfortunate raving mad before he dies in agony.[30]

Kung Bushmen of the Dobe region shoot poisoned arrows or throw poisoned spears in public duels and occasionally hit bystanders, including women and children. The poison can kill a man in about six hours, and attempts to remove the poison, by sucking, for example, are usually futile.[31]

The Akoa Pygmies of the Congo have formulated a complex and highly toxic arrow poison. Although they do attack enemies with it, their poison is designed as a hunting aid to paralyze the muscles and stop the heart of a wounded animal before it is lost in the dense jungle undergrowth. Ten kinds of plants are incorporated, among them two of the approximately two hundred species of *Strychnos* (Nightshade), one of *Strophanthus* (Poison Rope), one of *Erythrophloeum* (Sassy Bark), one of *Amaryllis,* and wild peppers. Wild yam juices and fig latex provide body and an adhesive quality.

The poison maker crushes the ingredients in a bowl into which he mixes his own saliva. When the liquid turns a brownish-red, he adds a marsh toad, whose skin is toxic, and boils the concoction until it thickens into a paste. He then adds crushed beetle grubs and black stinging ants, scrapes the paste from the bowl, and encloses it in soft bark, which he places in the body of a monkey, shot for the purpose, and buries. After several days of putrification, he exhumes the poison package and adds the sap of a euphorbia tree as a final adhesive.

The Akoa Pygmies have some of the most powerful arrow poisons in Africa. *Strychnos,* a tropical liana, provides strychnine, also a major ingredient in the infamous curare of the Amazonian Indians. The poison must contact blood to activate, but a slight scratch can cause fatality. The Indians of the Amazon often coated their fingernails with the sap of the *Strychnos* during hand-to-hand combat. When this poison is introduced into the blood, the muscles involved with breathing become paralyzed, and suffocation results.

The Poison Rope in the Akoa Pygmy recipe is also found in the arrow poisons of the native peoples of Senegal, Gambia, Guinea, and, in fact, most of the west coast of Africa. They mix the crushed seeds into a paste with saliva and set it in the sunlight for a few hours. The sap of euphorbia helps bind the poison to the arrow. Introducing this poison into the blood results in muscular paralysis, producing death and a condition difficult to distinguish from rigor mortis. *S. kombe* is the most popular of the genus *Strophanthus,* but *S. amboenis* (Omuhundure), *S. hispidus* (Inee), and *S. speciosus* (Common Poison Rope) are also prevalent. This arrow poison can kill a hippopotamus in twenty minutes. Although the sticky white latex collected from a cut in the bark of the euphorbia often serves as a poison adhesive, a few of the species, particularly *E. virosa* and *E. subsala,* are themselves toxic.

African arrow poisons, just as lethal although somewhat rare and limited in distribution, include *Adenium bohemians* (Desert Rose), *Asclepias stellifera* (Milkbush), *Buphane disticha* (Candelabra Flower), *Pachypodium lealii,* and *Abrus precatorius* (Rosary Pea). Genus *Amaryllis* comprises the notorious *A. belladonna* (Naked Lady), the bulb of which is poisonous to humans. The bark of *Erythrophloeum* contains the alkaloid erythrophleine, which affects the heart similarly to digitalis.

Woodchips from *Acokanthera spp.* (Bushman's Poison)—the most common species being *A. longiflora* (Apple Blossom Cassia), *A. oppositifolia* (Common Poison Bush), and *A. schmperi* (Poison Tree)—are frequently included as ingredients in making poison. The chips are boiled in water for as long as twelve hours or until a thick black paste forms. Tree gum becomes the adhesive. An arrow poisoned with *Acokanthera* can kill a large animal in fewer than twenty minutes.

Arrow poisons were used by the Tangale, Longuda, Borok, Pongo, Keri-Keri, Ngizim, Marghi, Lakai, Chibbuks, Dakkakerri, Ibibio, and Yoruba.[32] One scholar observed, "The Ibibio are the most expert poisoners on earth, though other Semi-Bantu tribes run them a close second. It is said that the Yoruba as well as Ibibio know drugs from which no effect will be visible for several months, but death is sure to result."[33]

Animal and vegetable toxins for arrow poison were known throughout the Sudan. The Hausa in east-central Africa based a complex arrow poison on *Strophanthus.*[34] The Akamba (central Bantu) traded poisons—

Acocanthera schimperiana, Adenium obesum (Elephant Foot) and *A. soma-
lense, Cassia spp. Crotalaria retusa* (Rattleweed), *Euphorbia spp., Securidaea
longipedouculata* (Little Tree), and *Tephrosia vogelii* (Fish Poison Bean)—
with their neighbors the Kikuyu, Embu, Tharaka, and Mijikenda. Contiguous groups who created arrow poisons from these ingredients include the Masaii, Wasania, Wakamba, Wanderobo, and Wa Nyika. The
Sakayes, Somangs, and Obok are also cited.

The Zulu poisoned their arrows and spears with an extract from the
root bark of *Combretum caffrum* (Cape Bushwillow). A scientific investigation of these poisons in the late 1970s determined that this poison
holds great promise in the treatment of solid tumor cancers. The investigators wrote,

> Unlike conventional tumor treatment, which often destroys healthy
> as well as cancerous cells, the Zulu poison targets only blood vessels
> formed inside tumors. Why the poison does this is still unknown.
> By shutting off the cells' supply of oxygen and nutrients, the poison
> stops a tumor thriving, and forces it into decline.[35]

Along the Indian Ocean coast of Kenya, the Giriama boiled the
branches of the *muriju,* a species of the *Acocanthera* group, to create a
sticky poison that quickly stops the heart. The Wakamba became the
major Kenyan elephant poachers by the 1970s with such poisons, which
can kill an elephant in a matter of hours. In Madagascar the roots, leaves,
flowers, and berries of the Tanghinia tree produce an effect like that of
Acocanthera, a poison primarily for warfare.[36] On the west coast of Africa, a seventeenth-century traveler noted, "When they are at war with
one another, they coat their arrowheads with poison which they make
from the sap of a certain green herb; but these poisoned arrows are not
allowed to be carried except in wartime."[37]

An 1800s account identified the Akus and the Somali of western
Africa as poison-arrow users.[38] Likewise, the warriors and hunters of
the west African kingdom of Benin (formerly Dahomey) made an arrow poison from *Strophanthus sarmentosus* (the source of cortisone) and
S. preusii (Twisted Flower) "with various kinds of nastiness added," including the gall of the drummer fish.[39]

References to poisoned arrows abound in the Islamic tradition. Since
the law of Muhammad forbade one Muslim from killing another, battles

involving Muslim contestants featured arrows designed not to kill but to engender sufficient pain to nullify the effectiveness of enemy fighters. In standard battle, two men rode a chariot, one driving and the other, with poisoned arrows or darts, sitting between the driver's feet facing backward.[40]

Many references to poison arrows come from Indonesia. The Javan tribes, as well as groups in Borneo, Sulawesi (Celebes), and Irian Jaya (western New Guinea), devised poison from the sap of the Upas tree. They considered *Upas tiute* the most potent of the genus but sometimes mixed *U. antiar* with it.[41] Borneo tribes, such as the Punan, coated blowgun darts with *Strychnos toxifera* (curare), *Antiaris toxicaria* (Ipoh Tree or Upas Tree),[42] and/or an unknown species of *Aconitum*.[43] On the Malaysian Peninsula, *Aconitum* was the choice for blowgun darts. In the Philippines, tribesmen covered their arrows with aconite poison,[44] and the Javans derived their poisons from *Antiaris toxicaria,* Upas, a tree of the mulberry and breadfruit family. The Karen people of Burma and the Mentawai of Siberut, Indonesia, have been adept at poisoning arrows for centuries. In Burma and Assam, the poison sources are varieties of *Antiaris, Strychnos,* and *Strophanthus.*

The Spanish left records of arrow poisoning by tribes in northern Mexico. The Jova put an amalgam of putrid cow livers, rattlesnake venom, centipedes, scorpions, and various poisonous plants on their arrow points. In the Caribbean, the Spanish confronted the Carib, whose arrow poison came from the sap of the Mancenilla tree (*Hippomane mancinella*),[45] one so deadly that, according to legend, the Indians tied captives to it to ensure a slow and horrible death. They also used *Hura crepitans* (Sandbox Tree), which is half a million times more toxic than potassium cyanide. The Arawak and Taino tribes doctored their wounds from poison arrows in warfare by covering them with a poultice of *Maranta arundinacea* (Arrowroot).[46]

Various authors reported Florida native peoples in possession of arrow poison. Ponce de Leon, when in search of the Fountain of Youth, is said to have died from a poisonous arrow wound. In 1521 another famous explorer, Ferdinand Magellan, was killed by a poison arrow on the island of Mactan in the Philippines.[47]

The native peoples of northern South America use curare, perhaps the best known arrow poison, for both warfare and hunting. The name is derived from their words *woorari, woorali,* or *urari,* all meaning "poison." Many variations exist, but the basic recipe contains *S. toxifera*, *S. guianensis*, *Chondrodendron tomentosum*, and *Sciadotenia toxifera*. To one, several, or all of the above could be added snake venom, poison ants, the root of the *hyarri*, or the secretion of several types of "Poison-Dart" frogs. To obtain its poison, the Indians agitate the frog until it secretes a white, frothy substance through its skin. The secretion from one frog can poison as many as fifty arrows, the lethality lasting on the tips for at least a year. The *Dendrobates azureus* is so deadly that just brushing against the frog's skin is enough to kill an adult.

A convention has arisen around naming a poison after the method of its storage. Curare made from *Strychnos* is stored in a calabash and that from *Chondrodendron* in a bamboo tube; hence, one hears of calabash curare or bamboo curare.

Indians evaluate curare potency in various ways. A common procedure involves pricking a toad with a curare-coated twig and counting the times it jumps before it dies. In one experiment archers, avoiding vital body organs, shot a large adult ox in the nose and both hips with three curare arrows. Within four minutes the animal was disoriented and staggering, and it died in twenty-five minutes.[48]

While one might assume that arrow poisoning is ancient history, such is not the case. Botanist Edward R. Ricciuti comments:

Witness the recent and bizarre spectacle of pygmy warriors carrying bows and poisoned arrows into combat alongside the Zairian army during the recent skirmishes with Katangese rebels in the Shaba region. Rebel soldiers who had routed the well-armed Zairian forces shuddered and lost heart at the news that the little men from the deep jungles were heading for the front.[49]

During World War II, Borneo and Malay tribesmen attacked Japanese forces with blowgun darts coated with *Aconitum*. The Balugas of Luzon joined the American forces against the Japanese armed with poisoned arrows,[50] and the Punan of Borneo killed many Japanese invaders with *Strychnos* darts. Earlier in Java, local tribesmen fought the Dutch colonial administration with darts poisoned with *Upas*.[51]

The survey of military arrow poisoning has established that the practice is ancient, efficient, universal, and present as a potent weapon of warfare even in modern times. Some researchers, however, are of the opinion that arrow poisons are not native to Australia[52] whereas others note that Australian aborigines knew more than twenty poisons for fish and killed emus by poisoning their watering holes with the leaves of *Taphrosi purpurea* (Faux Indigo).

There is little mention in the relevant literature concerning arrow poison in warfare or hunting for classic Mesoamerican civilizations, such as the Aztec and the Maya, as well as Polynesia, yet numerous poisonous plants grew in the area. Perhaps this lack of weapon poisoning relates to elite combat where noble warriors fought close to their enemies with clubs and swords. Weapon poisoning seems to have predominated in areas where the bow and arrow was the typical weapon.

Because North American arrow-poisoning behaviors were quickly curtailed with the conquest of the New World, much of the documentation in the preceding survey was drawn from modern medical, botanical, and anthropological experts and must suffice to present a world context in which North American Indian practices can be evaluated.

Chapter 4

Arrow Poisons of the North American Indians

For clarity of presentation, the tribal groups germane to the theme of this chapter are organized in terms of the Culture Areas typically employed for Native North American ethnological discussion: Southeast, Northeast, Plains, Southwest, California, Great Basin, Columbia-Fraser Plateau, Northwest, Subarctic, Aleutian Islands, and Arctic.

The Northeast

The eastern boundary of the Northeastern Culture Area runs from Maryland, through New England, to Newfoundland and the southeast corner of Canada, and from the Atlantic seaboard to the lower Great Lakes. Major tribes of the area include the Iroquois Confederacy (Seneca, Cayuga, Onondaga, Oneida, and Mohawk) and the Huron, Algonquin, Penobscot, Micmac, Erie, Abnaki, Naskapi, Montagnais, Menominee, and Delaware.

One of the earliest references to arrow poisoning in the Northeast comes from *Jesuit Relations: 1653–1654,* which notes that the Erie used poisoned arrows during their wars with the Iroquois in 1653–54.[1] The formula for the poison was not recorded though the assumption is that the arrows were infected with rattlesnake venom like those of the Indians in the West. French observers wrote that the Erie could fire eight to ten arrows before a musket could be loaded and that they could discharge a hail of poison arrows.[2] On July 20, 1654, the Iroquois charged an Erie fort, but the Erie's poisoned arrows kept them at bay.

The Seneca had poison arrows[3] as did the Micmac, whose arrows were tainted with a preparation of bark, root, and a bush, the identity of which is not known (or was not revealed).[4] And of the Oneida, an observer wrote that they killed poisonous blue otters and carefully preserved the meat.

A famous legend recounted by the Illini Indians describes an encounter between the tribe and a monstrous, dragon-like bird, which they called the Piasau, "the bird that devours men." In 1673 Father Jacques Marquette saw a cliff painting of the creature outside present-day Alton, Illinois, during his descent of the Mississippi River and described it in his journal. According to the legend, after his village was savagely attacked by the Piasau, a famous chief named Ouatoga secluded himself to pray for guidance. The Great Spirit instructed him to arm a hundred warriors with arrows that had been dipped in copperhead venom, and the hideous monster was destroyed. For generations thereafter, when Indians passed the cliff where the battle had taken place, they fired arrows or guns in commemoration of the great victory.

The Southeast

The Southeast Culture Area stretches from Florida to Maryland and from the Atlantic coast to the Mississippi River. The Cherokee, Creek, Chickasaw, Choctaw, Seminole, Powhatan, Catawba, and Rappahannock occupied this territory.

Many early explorers and settlers in the Southeast had something to say about local Indians poisoning arrows. French planter Antoine Le Page Du Pratz, who lived in the immediate vicinity of the Natchez in the early 1700s, wrote in *Histoire de La Louisiana,* "Another creeper is called by the native doctors 'the medicine for poisoned arrows.' It is large and beautiful. Its leaves are quite long and the pods which it bears are thin, about one inch wide and eight to ten inches long."[5]

Another early 1700s writer commented that the North Carolina Indians had "a certain method in poisoning their arrows, and they will temper them so as to work slow or swift as they place; they can make it so strong that no art can save the person or beast that is wounded with them, except it be their kings and conjurers, their young men being ignorant of it."[6]

Almost a century earlier, Gabriel Archer wrote that Indians he met in the vicinity of what is now Richmond, Virginia, "gave me a root wherewith they poison their arrows." They also showed him an herb, which they called *wisacan,* which was an antidote for the arrow poison. In 1687 Reverend John Clay, traveling among the Indians of Virginia, wrote a friend, "There are traditions of their having an art to poison their darts, but I could never find any solid ground for that report."[7]

Frank G. Speck, in his authoritative *Chapters on the Ethnology of the Powhatan Tribes of Virginia,* notes, "A tradition is related by the Mattaponi concerning the poisoning of arrowheads by their ancestors. It is said by a Powhatan Major there that the stone arrowheads with a flat side, and especially those with corrugated edges, were intended to carry a poison made from rattlesnake venom glands mixed into a paste."[8]

One of the tribes of the Powhatan Confederacy, the Chickahominy, developed an arrow-poisoning tradition that spanned even into modern times. O. Oliver Adkins, Chickahominy chief in the mid-1900s, had this to say in a letter to Frank Speck in February 1943:

> First would kill deer, take liver. Then would capture a dangerous snake, like a copper head. Hold him with a forked stick so he could strike liver. Held up before until he was exhausted. Then if that wasn't enough poison in liver, another was captured. When enough poison was in liver, then the liver was beat up in a pulp or glue form, and the arrow would be dipped in that glue, and any animal that was hit by this arrow and it crack the skin he would die. This was practiced up to the middle 1800s by the Adkins, Bradby, and Jefferson families. It was told to me by one of my older councilmen who is almost 70 years old, and it was told to him by his father.[9]

The Chickahominy and Rappahannock's method of arrow poisoning was perhaps the most widespread in North America. Minor variations existed from one group to another—as seen in those of the Chickahominy and Rappahannock—but two ingredients always appeared: snake venom and rotten organic matter. The Seminole of south Florida were observed employing this technique.[10]

The Big Cove Band of the Cherokee in Swain County, North Carolina, poisoned their arrows by chewing a root and applying the juice. While captive of the Catawba in South Carolina in 1755, Colonel James Smith witnessed their arrow poison,[11] and Danila Padilla, an early Creek observer, wrote that the Georgia Creek dipped their arrows into "some very poisonous and deadly substance."[12]

Indians from Florida to Quebec, west to California, and throughout the Rocky Mountains used a paste of the partially developed seeds of *Co-*

nium maculatum (Poison Hemlock) to poison arrows.[13] The Koasati of Alabama, members of the Creek confederacy, believed strongly in the power of *Eryngium virginianum* (Bear Grass), and both they and the Alabama tribes thought that merely striking an enemy with this plant would kill them.[14] The Mikasuki Seminole of southeast Florida believed that they could poison their arrows with special songs.[15]

The Southwest

The Southwest Culture Area covers most of New Mexico and Arizona, northern Mexico, and the southern half of Utah and Colorado, where a number of cultural traditions thrive. The Navaho occupy the north-central part, and to their south their linguistic relatives, the various Apache groups, hold sway. The Pueblo tribes (the Zuni, Hopi, and Laguna) inhabit the central regions, and to the west and southwest live a variety of smaller horticultural groups (the Pomo, Pima, Mohave, and Havasupai).

Navaho and Apache arrow-poison traditions have been thoroughly documented probably because hostile contact with them, beginning with the Spanish incursion into their area in the early to mid-1400s and continuing into relatively modern times, brought their weaponry to the attention of soldiers and military medical practitioners.

The Navaho prepared several variations of the snake-venom–rotten-meat poison. In *Ethnobotany of the Navaho,* Francis H. Elmore wrote, "A rattlesnake was first caught and killed on a rock. Next a yucca (*Yucca spp.*) leaf was heated over a fire and the juice squeezed onto the blood of the snake. Finally charcoal made from the pith of this cactus was added. The arrows were then painted from the point to about six inches back up the shaft." [16] *Usnea barbata* (Alpine Lichen) provided the base for another Navaho arrow poison. They mixed a hot infusion of this plant with decayed sheep, cow, or antelope spleen and buried it near a fireplace until it thoroughly decayed, then applied it to the arrowheads.[17]

A mixture of *Rhus toxicodendron* (Poison Oak), *Phacelia crenulata* (Wild Heliotrope), *var. ambigua* (Northern Red Oak), charcoal from a lighting-struck tree, and deer blood was recorded,[18] as was a compound of *Opuntia polyacantha* (Plains Pricklepear), *Yucca glauca* (Small Soapweed), and *Toxidodenron radicans* (Eastern Poison Ivy).[19] The Navaho created an antidote with *Eupatorium purpureum* (Joe Pye Weed).[20]

A Hopi story about a raid on a Navaho dance mentions Navaho poison making, as well as the relationship between armor wearing and poison arrows.[21] The story claims that the Navaho prepared poison by sus-
pending a dead rattlesnake over a vessel, into which the putrid matter
from the decaying snake dropped. They mixed this with poison extracted from the fangs of the snake and applied it to their arrows. The
story continues with the Hopi reshooting the arrows that the Navaho
had shot at them. The Hopi wore wrappings of buckskin, a kind of soft-
armor, and were little affected by the arrows, but many of the Navaho
wore no armor and died.[22]

An Apache arrow analyzed in 1871 showed evidence of rattlesnake
blood corpuscles and a crystalline substance identical with viperine or
crotaline, the active ingredient of its venom. In some instances their arrow poison included crushed red ants, centipedes, and scorpions. The
Lipan Apache dipped their arrows in the sap of the *Y. angustifolia,*[23] and
the Chiricahua Apache combined rotting animal blood and prickly pear
spines. One researcher felt that the latter concoction had no inherent
potency; rather, it originated from the incantations of the shaman
preparing it. The western Apache had *eh-ehstlus,* a mixture of spit, deer
spleen, and nettles left to rot before being painted onto arrow points.

A number of Apache elders offered the following information concerning arrow poisons:

> Our people used to use poison on their arrows, both in war and in
> hunting. This poison was made from a deer's spleen. This was dried
> first, then ground up fine and mixed in with the ground roots or
> stalks of nettles and also some plant that has a burning taste, like
> chili. The mixture is put in a little sack made from a part of the
> deer's big intestine.
>
> Then when all is ready, the maker spits into the bag and ties it
> up tightly and quickly so that none of the bad air will escape. The
> bag is hung from a tree for about three days till good and rotten
> and in liquid form.
>
> If the poison gets dry and hard it can be ground up and mixed
> on a stone with spit, just as paint is. This is bad poison and if you
> just have a scratch and get this in it, you will swell up all over.
> When a poison arrow is shot into a deer, no matter if it merely
> scratches him, he will die in about eighty yards.[24]

Another informant added that sometimes they added a species of lichen which grew on particularly heavy rocks, the purpose being to magically mimic the sensation of large stones within the victim's body. And another contributed that while preparing this poison, a man must ensure that children and dogs do not come near it. He added that he included sand in his version.[25]

An Apache informant told of an arrow poison that they previously made from a kind of insect. This is novel, though the Bushmen's use of a particular bug for poison might be considered, as well as the not-uncommon variety of scorpions, spiders, ants, and centipedes in many arrow poisons worldwide. Even the bug-based poison, however, was buried for several days.[26]

The Laguna Pueblo concocted an arrow poison from "snake venom and mud" so dangerous that even a scratch from a point treated with it could kill.[27] Other Pueblo peoples were also cited for arrow poisons. In 1862, physician J. B. Hill gave a Hopi recipe, yet another variation on the venom—putrid meat theme.

> They exposed the liver of a small animal to the fangs of a rattlesnake. After the venom had been infused, the organ was removed, wrapped in the animal's skin and buried for about a week. It was then resurrected, and the points were dipped in the rotting mess. When the projectiles were dry, they were dipped in blood, and again dried, and preserved for use.[28]

The Isleta Pueblo people made arrow poison from *Chrysothamnus nauseosus* (Rabbitbush) and arrow shafts from the fragile *Atriplex canescens* (Fourwing Saltbush), which always broke off inside the body.[29]

Acoma Pueblo warriors used *Ranunculus spp.* (Buttercups) for arrow poison.[30] Some of the Pueblo Indians attached arrow points dipped in blood to the bodies of their stone fetishes, a magical practice which they called "the Lightning."

In *The Journey of Coronado,* we find reference to early Pueblo Indian poison. Diego de Alcaraz, though directed to capture a Pueblo chief and his entourage, released them for ransom of cloth and other items needed by the Spanish troops. "Finding themselves free, the Indians renewed the war, and as they were strong and had poison killed several Spaniards and wounded others so that they died on the way back."[31]

The arrow poison of the Moqui of Utah came from an animal liver bitten by a rattlesnake and left to putrefy.[32] They buried the liver in the skin of the animal from which it was taken for seven or eight days, then the Moqui applied the poison to the arrow and allowed it to dry. Finally, they coated the arrow in animal blood and again dried it before it was considered ready for use.[33]

The Havasupai, who farmed along the floor of the Grand Canyon, created a number of arrow poisons. For one they boiled the leaves of *Ptelea trifoliate* (Common Hop Tree).[34] One of their most complex recipes follows:

The poison (*paisa'ha*) was of a black substance in the big scorpions, centipedes, red ants. *Matginyue* (a small back biting bug), jimson weed, and *quagamuna* (a weed growing on the canyon bench). These are mashed, dried, and stored. Soapweed leaves are thrown into the fire to get hot, and wrung to expel the juice. The little finger is wet with this glue, dipped in the powder, and a little is put on arrowhead and fore shaft. A mere scratch is sufficient to kill.[35]

Regarding warfare between the Lower Pima of Sonora and the Apache, David M. Brugge, a specialist in Pima ethnography, wrote, "A poison was prepared from the juice of a plant [possibly *Euphorbia spp.*] mixed with the pulp of prickly pear stem segments. The wooden arrow points were soaked in this long enough for the wood to absorb the poison and remain deadly for a considerable period."[36] Another source adds, "When going on a scout against the Apache Indians, their bitter foes, the Pimas frequently dip the points of their arrows in putrid meat, and it is said that a wound caused by such an arrow will never heal, but fester for some days and finally produce death."[37]

Use of poisoned arrows by the Opata of Sonora has been documented. A soldier in Coronado's expedition received a slight scratch on his hand from one of them and was dead two days later. Coronado lost seventeen men in Sonora because of them. Pedro de Castaneda de Nagera, traveling with Coronado in 1540, commented that the men would die in agony from only a small wound. He described one case in which the skin of the soldier struck by the poisoned arrow "rotted and fell off until it left the bones and sinews bare, with a horrible smell."[38]

Along the southern borders of the Southwest Culture Area, the

Cahita had poisoned arrows.[39] The Spanish military and mission documents often mentioned Seri poisons. They employed a variety of plant ingredients, including *Marsdenia spp.*, *Jatropha cinerea*, *J. cuneata*, and *Euphorbiaceae spp.* The major ingredient in all of their arrow poisons was *Sapium biloculare* (Mexican jumping bean).[40]

The tribes of the lower Colorado River preferred the following methods:

> Some of the tribes poisoned the arrow tips and claimed that they could kill people from the effects of the poison alone. Yavapais pulverized a mixture of rattlesnake venom, spiders, centipedes, a variety of long-winged bee, and walnut leaves. They bagged this mixture in deerskin and buried it in hot ashes for a day, thus rotting some of the ingredients. They hung the mixture up to dry until it was smeared on the arrow points.[41]

All Western Apaches used arrow poison in warfare. Its presence is noted for the Northern Tonto, San Carlos, Southern Tonto, Cibecue, and White Mountain. An Apache from Canyon Creek described the process for making arrow poison that had been passed down in his family:

> A small internal organ "like a stocking" from the top of a cow's stomach was hung until it rotted. Wasps were caught and held against this rotted organ until they stung it. Then pigeon blood was added. The material was kept for about two weeks, then mixed with burnt cactus spines. The substance was then placed on arrows and spears, both point and shaft to a total length of four to five inches. A mere scratch by an arrow so treated was reputed to cause a deer to swell up and die.[42]

The California Area

The California Culture Area corresponds to the present-day state with the exception of parts of the south, which more efficiently fit the Southwest Area culturally, and zones in the northwest, which better match Northwest Coast cultural patterns. Tribes in the western regions shared many cultural traits with those of the adjacent Great Basin area. Major tribal groupings in the northern parts comprised the Shasta, Karok,

Achumawi, Konkow, Pomo, Yurok, Hupa, and Yuki. The central region was occupied by the Miwok, Yokuts, and Esselen Costanoan while the Chumash, Gabrielino, Serrano, Cahuilla, Luiseno, and Ipai were found in the south.

In southern California, poisoned arrows were reported for the Gabrielino,[43] the Cahuilla,[44] and the Chumash;[45] however, most references come from the crowded north. An interesting case involves the Pomo, who concocted an arrow poison, not for tactical advantage, but for magical attacks against their enemies. To the blood of four rattlesnakes, they added pulped spiders, bees, ants, and scorpions and either dripped the resulting liquid over an image of the enemy or painted it on an arrow, which they shot over his house. They rubbed the snake's eyes, which were removed prior to shedding while it was blind, on an abalone shell that they manipulated to flash light into their enemies' eyes, causing blindness.[46] In a fight with the Yokuts, the Kawaiisu treated their arrows with an unidentified weed they called *muguruva,* which effected nosebleeds.[47]

Arrow poisons are cited for the Maidu and Konkow.[48] The Southern Maidu would tease a rattlesnake with an animal until it struck several times. After the mashed liver decomposed, they painted it on arrow points, fore shafts, and sometimes spears.[49] Only village chiefs prepared the poison, which was not applied until immediately before use. The Maidu also embedded stone arrow points in wet *Evernia spp.* (Oak Moss Lichen) for as long as a year to poison them. Sometimes they added rattlesnake venom.[50]

Tolowa and Karok informants described smearing the juice of *Toxicodendron diversilobum* (Pacific Poison Oak) on arrow tips when hunting.[51] The same ingredient and application was recorded for the Yurok of Trinidad Bay.[52] In the summer of 1939, Karok informants related the tale of traditional Karoks dipping their arrows in rattlesnake brains before a fight.[53]

The Hupa did not poison their arrow points but constructed them from what they felt to be highly toxic flint collected from a quarry on the Mad River. This flint, when broken in a wound, would lead to a deadly infection.[54] They preferred to tip their war arrows with old points found around Howunkut village, which they thought to be extremely dangerous.[55]

Claiming that a light scratch from such an arrow would cause death, the Yuki of Round Valley in Northern California poisoned their arrows with *Equisetum telmateia* (Giant Horsetail Fern).[56] In Northern California, arrow poisons are reported for the Achumawi,[57] Klamath, and Modoc.[58] California Indians used *Piperacea* (American pepper plant), which "was gathered, dried and then ground in the rock mortar to a very fine powder, for use when our people exchanged poisoned arrows for bullets on the field of battle. Our positioned arrows were more effective than bullets, as a scratch would send an enemy to eternal rest."[59]

Some California Indians poisoned their arrows with *Evernia spp.*,[60] whereas others obtained poison from *Eremocarpus setigerus* (Turkey Mullen).[61] The Spanish referred to this plant as *yerba del pescado* (herb of the fish) because it was also used to stun fish. Several authors wrote that the Pit River Indians mixed dog's saliva with wild parsnip juice for arrow poison.[62]

The most common arrow poison of the Western Mono came from rotted deer liver that had been bitten by rattlesnakes and dried in the sun. They rubbed a small lump of the poison on a stone and smeared the powder on the arrow point. The arrows were kept in a special quiver beyond the reach of children. The poison worked slowly over a twenty-four-hour period, so deer injured by one of these arrows were trailed to where they eventually expired. The Western Mono made another arrow poison from plants that the informants could not identify.

The Southeastern Yavapai used poison arrows in warfare but not for hunting. To poison the arrows, they stuffed a piece of deer's liver with spiders, tarantulas, and a rattlesnake's head, wrapped it with yucca fiber, buried it, and maintained a fire over it. When rotten, it was exhumed, tied with string, and, because of its stench, hung from a tree far from camp. There it dried for several days and shrunk to only a fraction of its original size. Next, they rubbed a piece with a stone on a flat rock, adding a little water to form a paste. They rehung the unused portion, taking care to keep the paste from under their nails, lest they be poisoned.

A Yavapai elder recalled the case of a soldier who had been but scratched by a poisoned Havapai arrow that had passed through the sleeve of his heavy coat. He paid no attention to the scratch, but in two days his arm swelled, then the same side of his body. He eventually died.[63]

The Atsugewi thought that the flint points with which they tipped their arrows was poison in itself. For warfare, however, they applied concocted poisons to their arrows. The simplest poison involved burying a deer liver or pancreas, allowing it to rot, and then applying the putrefied results to the arrow. A more complex arrow poison was made from a deer pancreas, the gall of a coyote, the air bladder of a fish, red paint, and rattlesnake teeth. The concoction was then mixed in a mortar and permitted to rot before being applied to the arrow or spear points. Another Atsugewi informant told of a method of creating poison in which rattlesnake heads and chopped-up roots of wild parsnip were put in a skin with a handful of arrow points, and allowed to rot before attaching the treated arrows.[64]

A poison of unknown source, called *pohil* by the Tubatulabal, was applied to both war and hunting arrows.[65]

Ishi, the last of the Yana of California, recounted that his people made arrow poisons, as so many North American Indians did, by infusing a deer liver with rattlesnake venom. They decocted the leaves of *Bertholletia spp.* (American Arrow Wood) to counteract poisoned wounds suffered in battle.[66]

The Great Basin

The Great Basin Culture Area lies within the state of Nevada and parts of Idaho and southeastern California. The major cultural entities were the Ute, Paiute, Paviotso (Northern Paiute), Panamint, Washo, Gosiute, Shoshone, and Bannock.

When Lewis and Clark encountered the Shoshone, they were told of two types of arrow poisons. In the first case, the Shoshone simply applied rattlesnake venom to their arrowheads. In the second, they incorporated crushed ants into a paste with an animal's spleen and set the compound in the sun to decay. When thoroughly putrefied, it was applied to arrows for war and hunting. They assured Lewis and Clark that, if an arrow so treated merely broke the skin, it would cause certain death.

The arrow poisons of the Gosiute, who ranged in modern-day Utah and Nevada, were from *Erigeron grandiflorus* (Large Flower Fleabane), *Valeriana dioica* (Marsh Valerian),[67] and *V. sylvatica* (Woods Valerian).[68] They also were aware of the very poisonous *Cicuta douglasii*.

The Northern Paiute frequently poisoned arrows for warfare and big-game hunting. Their *akwatsi* was said to take effect immediately, causing swelling around the wound.[69] Game thus killed was edible without excising areas adjacent to the puncture, as was the case with many other hunting poisons. The preparation of *akwatsi* is described in the following account by a Northern Paiute:[70]

> Our poison is made from the deer's *akwatsi,* a black looking stuff on the intestines which looks like the liver but is smaller. Cook it in the ashes and let it dry. It smells bad. Stick the arrow point in, let it dry, or rub the poison with the finger. There is no cure, so you have to be careful, especially if your finger is cut.

For a second Northern Paiute arrow poison, they mashed *Cicuta spp.* and simply pushed the root-paste until the tip was damp and then dried it.[71] This poison was considered so deadly that they used it against enemies but never when hunting game that they planned to eat.[72]

The Columbia-Fraser Plateau

The Columbia-Fraser Plateau Culture Area stretches north of the Great Basin into the southern edges of British Columbia. It is roughly bound on the east by the Rocky Mountains and on the west by the Sierra Mountains. The western reaches are influenced by Northwest Coast and California cultures, and the east by the Plains culture. Important tribes include the Nez Perce, Cayuse, Yakima, Klamath, Cowlitz, Thompson, Okanagan-Colville, Spokane, and Salish.

The Interior Salish[73] and the Nez Perce rubbed rattlesnake venom on their arrows, and the Nez Perce also applied simple venom.[74] In some cases, the Interior Salish mixed rattlesnake venom with the crushed flowers of *Ranunculus spp.*[75] The Salish considered obsidian projectile points to be "poisonous."[76]

Moerman notes that the Thompson Indians of British Columbia created arrow poison with *Artemisia dracunculus* (Wormwood), *Cornus sericea* (Red Osier Dogwood), and *Ranunculus sceleratus* (Celery Leaf Buttercup).[77] The latter was thought to be so poisonous that sometimes the arrow was considered sufficiently poisoned after having been rubbed with the plant, but the crushed flowers were also mixed with rattlesnake venom.

The Klamath stirred the mashed roots of *C. masculatum* with rattlesnake venom and decomposed deer liver. After the mixture rotted, they dipped arrows into it and dried them over a low fire. During the last step they offered prayers, which were believed to augment the efficacy of the poison.[78]

The Okanagan-Colville coated their arrowheads with pulverized *Zigadenus venenosus* (Death Camas) roots or dipped them into the powdered roots of *C. douglasii*. During her fieldwork, Nancy Turner, an ethnobotanist investigating the use of poisons by Native Americans, handled the root without gloves and suffered a violent reaction in which her face and hands became inflamed and swollen.[79] In addition, David Moerman has stated that the Okanagan-Colville poisoned arrows with *Ranunculus glaberrimus* (Sagebrush Buttercup).[80] The arrowheads were sometimes dipped into a pulp of mashed flowers and other times simply rubbed with the plant. They also soaked arrowheads overnight in a solution of mashed berry-laden juniper branches (*Juniperus communis*) in both hunting and warfare.[81]

The Upper Lillooet poisoned their war arrows with rattlesnake venom but did not add the *Ranunculus* flower, as did their Thompson neighbors. The Lower Lillooet did not use any form of poison on their arrows.[82]

The Great Plains

The Great Plains Culture Area is defined on the west by the Rocky Mountains, on the north by the gradual transition of short-grass plains to subarctic forest, on the south by the northern desert of Mexico, and on the east by the tall grass prairie. More simply put, it is the range of the American bison. The Blackfeet (a confederation made up of the Siksika, Kainah, and Piegan), Teton Sioux, Cheyenne, Crow, Arapaho, Kiowa, Comanche, Sarsi, Plains Cree, Assinboine, Osage, Pawnee, Ponca, Plains Apache, and Gros Ventre lived there; and all, to a greater or lesser extent, depended on the bison and the horse for their way of life.

The Blackfeet chewed *Cornus sericea* berries and spit the juice on the points of their war arrows, which they believed would lead to infection of arrow wounds.[83] The Gros Ventre, living on the northeast border of the Blackfeet, poisoned arrows by placing a small piece of *Cicuta spp.* on the shaft just behind the arrow point.[84]

The Sisseton Sioux combined the small spines of *Opuntia missouriense* (Prickly Pear) with grease and applied the thorny paste to their weapons.[85] They, like the Lipan Apache, who dipped their arrows into the sap of *Y. angustifolia,* believed that the spines had a mystic power to affect their enemies. The Teton Sioux, as well as the Siksika, Kainah, and Piegan, employed the widespread method of enticing a rattlesnake to attack a deer liver, buried the result until it putrefied, and coated their war arrows with it.[86]

The Cheyenne created with the leaves of *Potentilla fruticosa* (Shrubby Cinquefoil) what they considered their most potent arrow poison. They claimed that it went directly to the heart, thereby stopping it. When the Cheyenne and Sioux fought Custer on the Greasy Grass River, a Cheyenne priest, the Keeper of the Sacred Hat, wanted to use the poison against Custer, but none could be found growing in the area.[87] They included the same plant in rituals to attack their enemies magically. In the same fashion, *Actaea rubra* (Red Baneberry) was intended to blind their enemies. The root of this plant, called "sweet medicine" by the Cheyenne, was chewed and blown, first in the four directions, then toward the enemy.

Omaha arrow poison came from the root of an unidentified vine, to which was added the decaying flesh of a lizard and a "bug that swims on the surface of the water."[88] Arrows tainted with this poison were not for warfare or hunting, however, but for a legal trial, where an arrow was shot into a ritual effigy as one of the final acts.

The Plains Cree did not use poison arrows though "magical concoctions" were applied to arrowheads to make them more efficacious.[89] Finally, the Tonkawa in southern Texas believed that the juice of the mistletoe leaf was an effective arrow poison.

The Northwest Coast

The Northwest Coast Culture Area extends north from the border of modern-day Oregon and California to the southwest coast of Alaska and encompasses Vancouver Island and the Queen Charlotte Islands. The western boundary is the Pacific Ocean and the eastern, the coastal ranges. Major tribes, whose staple of life is the salmon, are the Makah, Quinault, Nootka, Kwakiutl, Haida, Timshian, Bella Coola, and others. David Thompson, who explored the far West in the late-eighteenth and early nineteenth centuries, wrote the following about the Indians of the Columbia:

> The only natives that use poisoned weapons, are the scoundrels that possess this river from its mouth up to the first falls; to collect the poison, aged widows are employed. In each hand they have a small forked stick of about five feet in length, and with these the head and tail of the snake is pinned fast down to the ground. Then with a rude pair of pincers the fang teeth are gently extracted so as to bring the bladders of poison with them. The bladders are carefully placed in a mussel shell brought for this purpose.[90]

Thompson observed that these arrows looked as if they had been painted with a dark brown varnish. He agreed with the Indians about their potency. In one case, a man of his acquaintance was shot in the shoulder by an arrow that had not been recoated in poison in over five years. Still, "it affected his health," wrote Thompson, "and was supposed to have hastened his death."[91]

The Clallam of Puget Sound fashioned arrow points from copper obtained through barter with both Indian traders, whose sources ultimately reached north of the Great Lakes, and Europeans, who traded sheets of the material. In some cases, the copper that sheathed long-distance sailing vessels was scavenged from shipwrecks. The Clallam soaked their points in salt water until they corroded, knowing that arrow tips of this nature would leave very dangerous wounds.[92]

The Kwakiutl poisoned their arrows with *C. douglasii,*[93] while their neighbors, the Nootka, employed the root of *Veratrum viride.*[94] The Upper Stalo Indians of the Fraser Valley in British Columbia dipped their arrows in decayed human brains. In addition to poisoning arrows with *C. douglasii,* the Haisla and the Hanaksiala manipulated arrow poison magically. In the mid-1900s, when the tribes witnessed smallpox spreading in their direction, a shaman had a vision of four canoes filled with diseased spirits approaching. To counter them, he covered an arrow with hellebore roots and shot it toward them. The Haisla and Hanaksiala did not contract smallpox.[95]

The Far North

The Far North Culture Area comprises the subarctic forests of Canada, the Aleutian Islands, Kodiak Island, and the northern coastal realms of the Inuit of Canada and Alaska. Imperatives of aboriginal life were adaptation to extreme cold and expertise at hunting both sea and forest animals and fishing. No poisonous mushrooms, roots, or berries grew north of the timber line, and most plant products could be safely eaten. In the forests south of the treeline, however, a number of poisonous plants existed: *Cicuta spp.*, locally known as Musquash Root; *A. rubra; Amanita phalloides* (Death-Cup Toadstool); and *A. muscaria* (Fly Amanita Mushroom).[96] The Tutchone, Koyukon, Tanana, Chipewyan, Kaska, Slave, numerous Aleut groups, and a variety of Cree-speaking peoples inhabited this area. Many small Inuit bands lived along the western and northern coasts of Alaska, and tribesmen were found on Kodiak Island and contiguous islands.

In 1785, Catherine The Second, Empress of All the Russias, commissioned Commodore Joseph Billings to explore the "northern parts of Russia" to the American coast. He reached Kodiak Island and investigated around Cook Inlet. The expedition secretary, Martin Sauer, not only kept records mainly of a scientific, astronomical, and geographical nature, but also penned some interesting accounts of the indigenous peoples they encountered. While in the vicinity of Kodiak Island, he wrote,

> They also use poison to their arrows, and the Aconite is the drug adopted for this purpose. Selecting the roots of such plants as grow alone, these roots are dried and pounded, or grated; water is then poured upon them, and they are kept in a warm place till fermented; when in this state, the men anoint the points of their arrows or lances, which makes the wound that may be inflicted mortal.[97]

The Kanagmiut Inuit and Aleut dried and pulverized *Aconitum spp.* root, mixed it with a little water, and allowed it to ferment before applying it to their weapons.[98] The Aleut devised a unique version of a plant poison and decaying organic matter. Although not known in historic times, elders remember *Aconitum spp.*, as well as a poisonous amalgam of rancid human fat (sometimes brains were specified) and crushed bodies of small, poisonous worms from local freshwater lakes.[99]

The Aleut poisoned the "war darts" of their *atlatls,* or "spear throwers."[100] Russian explorer Ivan Evsieevich Popov Veniaminov observed their javelins in the early 1800s:

> Sometimes these were dipped in poison which was known only to a very few. When a javelin was flung at a man, it did not enter his flesh entirely but only the head with the point. The javelin head could be forcibly withdrawn from the man but the point always remained in him and consequently always brought a slow but certain death.[101]

In the forests south of Hudson Bay, the Cree poisoned arrows with the root of *Heracleum maximum.*[102] In fact, almost all North American Indian populations utilized biochemical poisons at the time of contact and well into the modern era. *Cicuta spp., Ranunculus spp., Veratrum viride,* and *Aconitum spp.* proved to be highly significant in the making of poison arrows, but a number of other plants and plant parts were also employed. Again, though a variety of preparation methods existed, the infusion of a liver by the repeated strikes of a rattlesnake and the subsequent putrification of the result prior to use was the most typical method.

Chapter 5

Other Uses of Poisons in Warfare

Although widespread arrow poisoning among North American tribes throughout all culture areas has been established, the issue of poisons in warfare is not yet exhausted. During the transition from bows and arrows to firearms, many North American Indian groups applied their arrow poisons to bullets. For a short span of history, some Native Americans apparently categorized both arrows and bullets as material projectiles and to some degree treated them the same way. For example, the Apache word for bullet is *ka,* or "arrow."[1]

The Tonkawa Indians of south Texas transferred their arrow poison, the juice of the mistletoe leaf, to the new weapon; however, rather than coating the bullets, as was most common, they dribbled the liquid down their gun barrels.[2] The Sisseton Sioux poked small holes in the bullet lead and pressed greased *Opuntia missouriense* spines into the perforations.[3]

Like the Sioux, the Blackfoot doctored their bullets and musket balls with traditional arrow poison.[4] The Cree south of Hudson Bay put a poisonous mush from *Heracleum maximum* on their bullets.[5]

As late as 1980, some Okanagan-Colville hunters still enhanced their bullets with juniper-based arrow poison.[6] Western Apaches covered musket balls with a compound of ground nettles, lichens, and rotten deer spleen—essentially the same recipe they had used on their arrows.[7] The Nootka of Vancouver Island poisoned their bullets with a paste of *Veratrum viride* root.[8]

Native Americans polluted the water supply of both game animals and human enemies.[9] Northwest Indians poured an infusion of crushed *Megarhiza oregana* (Oregon rock cress) roots into ponds or springs where deer drank, and the stupefied animals became easy prey. In the early days of Spanish contact, the Zuni poisoned the springs at the entrance to their valley with Yucca juice and unidentified cactus spines, which "caused suffering and death among the forces of Diego de Vargas."[10]

A generation later, an Indian leader named Opechancanough attempted to kill members of the first English expedition into Virginia by sending them tainted food. Captain John Smith wrote, "We find Opechancanough the last year [1621] had practiced with a King on the Eastern Shore, to furnish him with a kind of poison, which only grows in this country, to poison us."[11] Regarding English-Indian relationships along the central East Coast in the early 1700s, an account states, "A notorious shaman known as the Indian River Doctor brewed a large quantity of poison that was intended to be used to infect the drinking water of the colonists. A log house deeper in the swamp had been built as a repository for guns and ammunition, and a large quantity of poisoned arrows with brass points had been accumulated."[12]

Colonel James Smith reported on a poisoning technique of the Catawba Indians, a group with several novel methods of warfare. An Indian acquaintance described the Catawba tying buffalo hooves to their feet and walking after dark near an enemy village. The following morning, the villagers followed the tracks into a Catawba ambush. Smith wrote,

> In the morning those in the camp followed after these tracks, thinking they were buffalo, until they were fired on by the Catawbas, and several of them killed; the other fled, collected a party and pursued the Catawbas; but they, in their subtlety brought with them rattlesnake poison, which they had collected from the bladder that lies at the root of the snake's teeth; this they had corked up in a short piece of cane-stalk; they had also brought with them small cane or reed, about the size of a rye straw, which they made sharp at the end like a pen, and dipped them in this poison, and stuck them in the ground among the grass, along their own tracks, in such a position that they might stick into the legs of the pursuers, which answered the design; and as the Catawbas had runners behind to watch the motion of the pursuers, when they found that a number of them were lame, being artificially snake bit, and that they were all turning back, the Catawbas turned upon the pursuers, and defeated them and killed and scalped all those that were lame.[13]

A second account, this time from a Catawba informant, relates another instance of poisoned sticks:

The story goes that a large number of Iroquois were going toward a Catawba village. All of the able-bodied men of the tribe were away hunting. The young boys and the old men who had been left behind on hearing of the enemies approach, went to the medicine-man with the poisonous snake and asked him for poison. He took a bowl, held it before the snake and told the snake to give him poison. The snake, who was almost like a brother to the medicine-man, poured the venom into the bowl. Oak splinters about twelve inches long were cut and soaked in the venom. These splits were then put in the mud at various locations around the village, and so placed that about an inch of the splint, protruded. The Catawba attacked the Iroquois, and then feinted with a false retreat, leading the pursing Iroquois into the areas where the poisoned splints had been concealed. The Catawba were careful to skirt these areas, but the unsuspecting Iroquois were crippled and their ranks broken. The Catawba were then able to easily finish them off.[14]

In the Northwest Coast Culture Area, the Coastal Salish had to contend with the Kwakiutl, who often traveled as far south as Puget Sound on slave-raiding ventures. To protect themselves, they built highly sophisticated forts, one consisting of two plank houses within a stockade with tunnels leading to loopholes in the bank outside. Inside stood two poles upon which baskets of flaming pitch could be hoisted to light the surrounding area at night, and sharp sticks soaked in rattlesnake poison were hidden outside the walls in the grass.[15] The Yaqui of northern Mexico "were known to sow trails with thorns poisoned with a venom so strong that there was no antidote."[16]

Poisoning was a typical means of assassination among North American Indians, and they knew dozens of plants with which they could contaminate the food or water of an enemy. Poisoning was greatly feared, according to a number of sources. The Aleut, for example, laced their adversaries' food with the juice of *Ranunculus occidentalis* or *Equisetum*.[17]

Captain Smith recounted an attempt by Wecuttanow, a Powhatan chief's son, to poison him,[18] and members of his own tribe poisoned the Pequot renegade Wequash for assisting the English in the Pequot War.[19] North Carolina Indians were known to poison potential chiefs whom they judged incapable of governing.

The Iroquois concealed dried and powdered *Eupatorium perfoliatum*

(Common Boneset) in an enemy's liquor flask, the Western Keres added pulverized *Datura wrightii* to water, and the Menominee sprinkled dried *Comptonia peregrina* (Sweet Fern) leaves on an enemy's food. The neighboring Meskwaki adulterated food with finely chopped root of *Arisaema triphyllum* (Jack in the Pulpit), and the Penobscot used *A. triphyllum* in the same fashion. The Lakota preferred *Zigadenus venenosus* as a murder weapon.

A questionable report—in that no other such account appears in the voluminous literature on North American Indian ethnobotany—by Huron H. Smith, noted for his ethnobotanical studies among tribes of the Great Lakes region, mentions that *Sisyrinchium campestre* was mixed with oats to make horses sleek and vicious.[20] The ingestion of this plant rendered their bites poisonous, a handy trait for a war horse. Dogs were given *Clintonia borealis* to poison their teeth for hunting and fighting.[21] A Navaho source mentioned that powdered *Datura spp.*, when thrown in the face of an enemy, was an effective weapon.[22]

The novel use of botanicals among the Makah should be noted. They pounded the fresh roots of *Rumex obtusifolius* (Bitterdock) to rub on their bodies when near a powerful enemy. Warriors believed that this medicine would prevent them from serious injury in battle and was so important that they would pay from five to ten blankets for one application.

The most striking fact in the preceding materials is that Native American Indians could wage war with poisons delivered to their enemies in a great variety of ways, though the poisoned arrow was the most common. The wide range of techniques used in poison manufacture suggests that they had been experimenting with biochemical poisons for a long time. The use of poisons may indeed date to the earliest peopling of the New World.

Chapter 6
Paleo-Indian Poison Use

The people referred to by North American archaeologists as the Paleo-Indians, or "ancient Indians," perhaps exhibit the first evidence of projectile-point poisoning by Native Americans. Precisely when these first Americans entered the New World and where they originated continues to be hotly debated.[1]

The most widely accepted notion, however, is that the ancestors of the American Indians migrated from northeast Asia in small hunting and foraging bands more than 12,000 years ago by way of a land bridge that was exposed between Siberia and Alaska during the last glaciations. A minority of archaeologists champion northern and western Europe as one of the possible origin points whereas traditional Native Americans claim that they evolved in the New World.

Those who tout the Bering Strait land-bridge route—and most do—should consider that the strait can be crossed during winter when the water freezes over. Only fifty-five miles separates Siberia from Alaska at the narrowest point, and today a cottage industry on the Alaskan side equips and supports daredevil expeditions that have made the trek on everything from snowmobiles to jeeps to skis. In 1998 Russian Arctic explorer Dimitry Shaparov and his son Matvey encountered polar bears on their twenty-one-day journey on skis. Some decades back, another Russian expedition was air-lifted off the ice when twenty polar bears surrounded them. The presence of polar bears indicates that a large carnivore can find sufficient food for sustenance through an arctic winter, and it is supposed that human hunters could do likewise.

Agreement as to the precise time of the initial peopling of the New World is limited. The Tlapacoya site in Mexico has been dated between 24,000 and 21,000 years ago whereas the La Sena mammoth kill site in Nebraska contained 18,000-year-old bone collagen. The Cactus Hill site in Virginia revealed charcoal dated to more than 15,000 years ago. A persuasive new discovery, the Monte Verde site in Chile, has shown dates reaching back 12,500 years. Nevertheless, the essential debate continues.

Somewhat later than the dating of Monte Verde, unique fluted stone points in association with the remains of several species of mammoth were found at kill sites clustered on the southern plains of North America (Texas, New Mexico, Oklahoma) dating 11,500 to 10,900 years ago. Archaeologists refer to the Paleo-Indians responsible for these sites as the Clovis, after a New Mexico town near which the first materials were found.

The signature of the Clovis tradition is a projectile, or spear point, presumed to have been used in elephant hunting. The classic Clovis point is leaf-shaped with a channel, groove, or flute on one or both sides running from its base to about a third or half way to the tip. The points range in size from a little over one to five inches. The antiquity of these points, their origin, their function, and their manner of use are unknown. Some experts have suggested that the fluting provided a better "tongue-and-groove" fit for attaching the point to its shaft. The flute has been considered a "blood groove" to stimulate blood loss in the animal attacked while some have argued that the fluting lightened the weight of the stone point. Others have even imagined that they knew exactly how far up the point the string hafting material reached. Nonetheless, all is pure supposition, for the great age of the Clovis tradition precludes records of anyone having seen mammoth hunters in action with their fluted points.

The assumption that small groups of Clovis hunters attacked and killed the Columbian mammoth (*Mammuthus columbi*), the Jefferson mammoth (*Mammuthus jeffersonii*), the American mastodon (*Mammut americanum*), or the wooly mammoth (*Mammuthus primigenius*) with stone-tipped spears is problematic, though undeniable. The American mastodon stood eight to ten feet at the shoulder and weighed four to six tons. The Columbian mammoth was even larger, measuring twelve to fourteen feet at the shoulder and weighing eight to ten tons. The Wooly mammoth, larger still, averaged nine feet at the shoulder, weighed seven to nine tons, and was covered with guard hair as long as ninety centimeters. Add to this the thickness of the hide and fat and the massive bones needed to support such a tremendous weight, and these must have been intimidating animals for the Clovis hunters to confront. The contemporary Asian elephant, in contrast, stands six and a half to eleven and a half feet at the shoulder and weighs three to five tons whereas the African elephant measures ten to thirteen feet at the shoulder and weighs four to seven tons.

It is important to keep in mind the relative size difference between Clovis hunters and their mammoth and mastodon prey. A hunter who stood just under six feet (a generous estimate of Paleo-Indian stature) would reach only the mammoth's knee. The fluted points (several inches in length) with which they armed their spears would be mere splinters in the mass of these animals, perhaps equivalent to a pinprick on a human.

The mammoth's tusks and trunk also must be considered when imagining Paleo-Indians attacking a Columbian mammoth, for example. Most assume that such an attack would have been waged primarily with thrusting spears, which would require the hunter to be in close proximity. With the animal's trunk and tusks whipping from side to side, a trunk as big around as a man, and tusks as long as sixteen feet and as heavy as two hundred pounds each, however, the creature could effectively protect its throat and flanks from a human predator.

Another intriguing factor is that relatively few Clovis points have been discovered with the mammoths they killed. At the Dent site in Colorado, three Clovis points were found with twelve mammoths; at the Naco site in Arizona, eight were uncovered with one mammoth, four times the number found with any other mammoth. Typically only a few points accompany mammoth kills. It would seem, then, that if pure fire power with Clovis-point spears were killing the giant animals, many, many more points should be in evidence. Possibly the hunters recovered their points for further use or retrieved broken blades to be retooled into scrappers, cutting tools, or knife blades. Or, perhaps, they poisoned their points. When hunters in other parts of the world killed big game with poisoned weapons, they used very few points.

The Hunters, an anthropology film classic, is a documentary of a Kalahari Bushmen group and one of the few filmed demonstrations of big-game hunting with poisoned arrows. Early in the film, a hunter shoots a wildebeest with a small-tipped (about the size of a little-finger nail), unfletched arrow with poison painted just below the point. The animal is mortally wounded but harvested by lions before the hunter can track it. Later a similar arrow hits a giraffe, which the Bushmen track for several days. Too sick from the poison to flee the hunters, it stands while they hurl metal-bladed spears at its throat. The razor sharp spears either bounce off the thick hide or barely penetrate it and fall out. When the tip of one point enters the animal, it seems to have no effect. I have heard many anthropologists suggest that the filmmakers finally shot the beast rather than wait for the poison to finish its work as the Bushmen under normal circumstances would have done.

The Hunters makes several significant points. First, poison can kill large game animals. Second, it can be done with one small arrow. Even metal spear blades thrown at point-blank range have little or no effect on such a large animal, an animal that also is not fighting back.

It is possible that Paleo-Indian hunters who used fluted points against large game animals had poisons in their repertoire of hunting tools. Other observations support this assumption. Wherever contemporary "Stone Age" elephant hunters were found (predominantly Africa and India), they killed the animals with poisoned weapons, generally arrows. The Abor and Mishmis of India concocted a poison from several species of *Aconitum, Croton,* pig blood, cobra venom, and other unidentified toxic plants to slay elephants, tigers, and water buffalo. Their poison was effective on a two-and-a-half-ton elephant.

The Kung San of *The Hunters* fame killed big game in a matter of hours with poison from the *Chrysomelid* beetle. The Akoa Pygmy groups hunted elephants with arrows poisoned with *Strychnos, Strophanthus, Erythrophloeum,* and various animal and insect remains. They could bring down a hippopotamus in twenty minutes with a single arrow. In the 1970s, the Wakamba, the major elephant poachers in Kenya, designed poison from the boiled branches and bark of the *Acokanthera.* It seems reasonable that, if every other elephant-hunting population in the world employed poisons against the beast, the Clovis people did the same.

Claims that the fluting so diagnostic of the Clovis people has not been found outside North America are refuted by the Ainu of Hokkaido, Japan, who featured fluting on one side of their bamboo arrowheads. (Clovis points were sometimes fluted on only one side.) The Ainu hunter rubbed a pea-sized ball of poison into the flute, flush with the arrowhead's surface.

A criticism of one neither conversant with the bamboo found in Japan nor of the many ways it can be shaped and molded during and after the growing process might suggest that the Ainu fluted points were simply an accidental effect of splitting a hollow culm. However, a large spe-

cies of bamboo, generally referred to as "lumber bamboo" by Western-
ers, can grow culm walls half an inch thick or more. Such bamboos are
often shaped from their first emergence with a square dye composed of
four planks tied around the culm from the ground to six feet or more up
the new stalk. Much as binding splints of wood to a newborn's head in
cranial deformation, the bamboo binding will produce flat slabs, the
edges of which can be sharpened to a knifelike keenness.

In 1985, archaeologists Maureen L. King of the Desert Research Institute in Las Vegas and Sergei B. Slobodin of the Department of Edu-
cation in Magadan, Russia, reported in *Science* magazine, their find of
a Clovis-like fluted point at the Uptar site in northeastern Siberia. The
point was dated in reference to a volcanic level found beneath the point
at 8260 (plus or minus 330 years). A number of unfluted stone bifaces
that resemble Clovis points in basic shape were found nearby.[2]

The design of the Clovis points precludes bringing down the mammoth with force, which would have required larger points like the harpoon points used against whales. Simply, they were too short and too
fragile to be the sole killing force against a mammoth. The bone mass
and massive muscles with which elephants move tons of body weight,
combined with the constricted musculature of an animal under attack,
would shatter the delicate fluted points in the animal, and perhaps this
was intended. A number of early accounts indicate that some Indian
groups designed poison arrowheads to shatter or disengage from the
shaft within the victim's body. Thirteen such fore shafts have been found
at Clovis sites on the Wacissa and Aucilla Rivers in northern Florida.

The possible origin of Clovis populations also supports the poison-use
hypothesis. No one knows for sure where the Clovis people came from,
but experts presume northeast Asia, which suggests they traveled
through arrow-poisoning cultures into the New World. For example,
north of the Ainu, the native peoples of Kamchatka and the Kurile Island chain included *Anemone virginiana* (Virginia Wind Flower) and
Anemone nemorosa (Scarlet Wind Flower) in poisons for war and big-game
hunting. In northern China, arrow poisons, *A. japonicum* being the most
prevalent, have been around for millennia. Numerous species of *Aconitum* grow in the mountains of China, and hunters and warriors of Yunnan and Guangxi used arrow poisons well into the twentieth century.

Further east, the people of the Aleutian Islands had poison weapons.
Russian explorers document the presence of *Aconitum* in whale hunting

by the Aleut, as well as the Kodiak Islanders, and report that a single
thrust of a harpoon tainted with it could kill a whale. (Several decades
ago, European whale hunters experimented with cyanide and other poisons in whale hunting.)

The most likely candidate for the major poison of the Paleo-Indian
mammoth hunters is *Aconitum spp.*, recorded in China, Mongolia, and
Siberia—the probable origin of the Paleo-Indians. In the North Pacific
area, such groups as the Aleut and the Kodiak hunted whales with it, a
testimony to its lethality against large mammals.

Though *Aconitum spp.* favors moist, cool soil, remnant populations
still grow in New Mexico, Colorado, Wyoming, and Montana, the area
that supplies some of the earliest evidence of Paleo-Indian mammoth
hunters. At the time of the Clovis tradition, the Great Plains and Southwest had the cool, damp conditions that *Aconitum spp.* prefers.

The ethnohistorical, ethnobotanical, and ethnological evidence—
along with the limited number of points found at Clovis kill sites, the
comparison with Stone Age elephant hunters worldwide, the arrow
fluting of the Ainu, the flute point found at the Uptar site in Siberia, and
the poison-laden cultural environment that must have been the seat of
the Clovis tradition—suggests that the Clovis hunters used poisoned
points, at least some of the time, to kill mammoths. No other explana-
tion exists except that based on pure speculation.

It must be acknowledged that poisons were one of many ways big
game was taken. Hundreds of thousands of years before the advent of the
Paleo-Indians, Old World hunters (*Homo erectus*) drove animals into bogs
and ravines and over cliffs with fire. Some African Pygmy populations
rigged weighted elephant spears to fall with great force into the animals'
heads or backs. The fluted point should be considered a type of projectile point, not the be all and end all of the Clovis mammoth-killing arsenal. Poisons may not have been required for mammoth calves, elders,
or injured individuals.

Around 11,000 years ago, a major climatic change dried the moist
savannahs where the Clovis hunters roamed. The temperature warmed,
and the mammoth became extinct. So too did the Clovis tradition,
which gave way to a similar way of life called Folsom, named after a
town in New Mexico near which the first Folsom points were found.
Folsom culture resembled Clovis in a number of ways. Centered in the
same general area, both were associated with fluted points and big game

animals. For Clovis it was the mammoth; for Folsom, *Bison antiquus,* the much larger forerunner of the modern *Bison bison.*

Folsom points were smaller (one to three inches) than Clovis and more detailed. The Folsom flute, however, is much longer and deeper, running two-thirds of the way from the base to the point, and like Clovis, sometimes fluted only on one side.

Bison antiquus was a formidable target. It was—extrapolating from what is known of *Bison bison*—very intelligent, unpredictable, incredibly strong, and agile. To make matters more challenging, it ran in herds numbering into the thousands. *Bison antiquus* stood about seven and a half feet at the shoulder and weighed approximately 2,400 pounds. The distance between horn tips was four and a half feet, and one species' horns measured six feet or more.

Modern Bison can run at sustained speeds of thirty miles-per-hour and maintain forty-five for short distances. They are excellent swimmers, even crossing water barriers a kilometer wide. They can jump six feet vertically and seven horizontally. Whereas a typical cattleguard spans about seven feet, because of the bison's jumping ability, those on bison ranches are often fourteen feet. Bison were so dangerous and powerful that, though the Plains teamed with wolves and grizzly bears, none focused on it as a major food source.

The capabilities of bison, particularly their speed, suggest another reason for the development of longer flutes on Folsom points as compared to those of Clovis. Poisoned arrows prevent prey from running a great distance before dying, a particularly important condition in rough terrain or thick forests. The kill attempt depicted in *The Hunters* illustrates that, if the wounded animal distanced itself from the hunter, predators could find it first.

In considering the environment of the Folsom hunters and *Bison antiquus,* one might say that the above qualifications do not apply. The Plains, for the most part, are flat and the terrain uncluttered. But, because of the bison's speed and ability to swim and jump impressive distances, coupled with the difficulty of tracking an animal traveling with a herd leaving thousands of hoof prints, the Folsom hunters would have needed poison to prevent the animal from outdistancing them. Thus, the flutes are larger; that is, they may have carried heavier loads of poison. The smaller points created more efficient spear-thrower darts, ones not so heavily weighted forward like larger Clovis type. They were more efficient for throwing atlatl darts greater distances at running bison whereas long-distance shooting was unnecessary for mammoth hunters. The idea that Folsom hunters developed the spear thrower is pure conjecture, though a commonly held surmise.

The fluted traditions on the southern Plains faded with the rise of the Plano traditions (10,000 –7,000 years ago). It is assumed that by this time the Plains people hunted in large semitribal groups. The use of poisons continued, as is witnessed from their near-universal presence at the time of contact. Over the thousands of years that must be considered, the ancient Indians perhaps refined their poisons, leading to a diminished need for fluting as lighter applications sufficed to maintain killing power. Most were so potent at the time of contact that a relatively small amount could kill or maim.

Archaeology cannot confirm or deny poison use by Paleo-Indians. The evidence is circumstantial, though thought-provoking. A surface analysis of Clovis and Folsom fluted points might reveal the presence of poison; then again, finding poison residue after thousands of years in the moist environment typical at the time of the great mammoths is unlikely.

Could Stone Age hunters have brought down an animal weighing many tons and standing three or more times the hunter's height? Yes. Does fluting exist in other parts of the world? Yes. When it occurs, is it associated with poisoning? Yes. Was the generally accepted northeast Asian origin of the Paleo-Indians home to hunting-poison users? Yes.

In 1999, paleo-archaeologist Gary Haynes presented a paper at a scholarly symposium that focused on the most current information available concerning the mixed fate of Clovis hunters and mammoths, particularly the notion that these hunters were responsible for the mammoth's extinction. He linked his work on modern elephant sites in Zimbabwe with what is known of the Clovis–mammoth relationship. The following is one of his many interesting observations:

And another point that often times is not raised when comparing the modern elephant population depletion during the ivory-hunting craze of 100 years ago is that, in spite of the fact that many elephant populations were driven to about zero—at least to a virtual zero point—during the ivory-hunting phases of the late 19th century in southern Africa, they've recovered to some of the highest densities anywhere in Africa within a hundred years. So elephants can recover from over hunting.[3]

Haynes then asks,

How could Clovis people, with spear points, have hunted an entire population of mammoths in North America to extinction if people with high powered rifles couldn't do it in the late 19th century?[4]

Perhaps the use of projectile-point poisoning by Paleo-Indians offers at least part of the answer.

Conclusion

Ethnobotanical and ethnohistorical sources clearly refute claims, proposed as recently as the late-twentieth century, that North American Indians rarely used arrow poison. The appendix lists the major North American groups and the poisons they used. The use of poisons was not relegated to one specific cultural or ecological zone but was, as the literature demonstrates, widespread in hunting and gathering as well as horticultural environments—in woodlands, deserts, subarctic forests, swamps, high plains, and mountains.

North American Indian arrow-poison usage resembles that of the bow and arrow–based cultures of Japan, China, eastern India, tribal Europe, South America, Africa, Indonesia, and Melanesia. There appears to be a relative dearth of its use in Polynesia and state-level Mesoamerica, which may relate to the presence of military nobles and codes of elite combat, and in the high arctic region, which could be explained by both ecological difficulties of plant growth at those latitudes and the armoring effect of thick parkas.

Although several authorities cited in the "Introduction" have concluded that poison arrows were neither widespread nor effective in Native North America, the appendix identifies more than eighty major tribes that used them. Perhaps these observers did not enter the literature on North American Indian ethnobotany or issued their comments prior to the development of the field. As for assertions that Spanish conquistadors exaggerated incidents involving poison arrows, their accounts coincide with those of French and English explorers in the Northeast and Russian explorers on the Northwest Coast, who documented these poisons in their respective territories of investigation.

Another area of misunderstanding may issue from the meaning of the word "poison," which I define in a military sense as a chemical substance capable of injuring, killing, or impairing an intended enemy combatant. Sometimes early observers looked at Indian arrow poison and did not see it. Robert Brown wrote of the California Indians in 1868, "They have, I may mention, no arrow-poison; but I have known some of the California Indians to get a rattlesnake, and irritate it until it had repeatedly struck into the liver of some animal impregnating it with its virus. They would then dip their arrows into this poisoned mess."[1]

A liver or spleen infused with rattlesnake venom and left to decay is one of the most common methods of creating arrow poison worldwide, a procedure the classical Greeks used with serpents. Concocting this type of poison is a technology, in that the various chemical and biological elements were not linked in nature but brought together for a specific purpose.

The term *biochemical* accurately describes the nature of many Indian poisons. In some cases, the arrow poison was strictly chemical—cicutoxin in *Cicuta spp.;* atropine, hyoscamine, and hyoscine in *Datura spp.;* and snake venom—and in others, strictly biological—bacteria from putrid meat, rotten blood, and decayed insects. The venom-infused, rotted liver, however, becomes a biochemical because it combines two deadly substances into one, and in this form the majority of arrow poisons were created.

The toxicity of rattlesnake venom, the venom most commonly employed by North American Indians in arrow-poison production, is based primarily on complex proteins. Of the many toxic elements present—including protease, phosphatidase, neurotoxin, cardiotoxin, hyaluronidase, and cholinesterases—protease disrupts local tissue and phosphatidase can cause motor and respiratory paralysis.

Venoms are so biochemically complex that only a few of the many found in the animal kingdom have been thoroughly analyzed. Snake venom is classified as either neurotoxic (affecting the nervous system) or hemotoxic (affecting the blood and body cells). Rattlesnake venom, a hemotoxin, is generally lethal to young children, the elderly, and those weakened by some chronic disorder; however, it causes extreme pain and destroys body tissue and affected organs. A venom-coated arrow entering the body equates a strike by a rattlesnake but is often worse because a victim of archers will likely be struck more than once.

In "Notes on Arrow Wounds," J. H. Hill wrote,

An expert bowman can easily discharge six arrows per minute, and a man wounded with one is almost sure to receive several arrows....

We have not seen more than one or two men wounded by a single arrow only. In three of our soldiers shot by the Navahos, we counted forty-two arrow wounds.[2]

In the mid-1800s, George Catlin observed Apache warriors practicing archery from running horses and wrote, "The rapidity with which their arrows are placed upon the string and sent is a mystery to the bystander, and must be seen to be believed. No repeating arms ever yet constructed are so rapid."[3]

In the autumn of 1539, a Spanish expedition under Hernando De Soto attacked the Indian stronghold of Mabila, somewhere in present-day Alabama. After the battle, his secretary, Rangel, reported that 22 Spaniards had been killed and 148 wounded. All told, they sustained 688 arrow wounds, many of the soldiers shot more than once.[4]

English longbowmen could fire ten to twelve arrows per minute. On May 19, 1852, in the Sanjusnagen-do of Edo, Japan, Masatoki, an archer in the service of the feudal chief Sakai, discharged 10,050 arrows, 5,383 hitting the center of the target, during 24 hours of uninterrupted shooting—an average of nine shafts per minute.[5]

The sheer volume of arrows that expert archers could release, coupled with the far-reaching use of their poisoning, is daunting. Even though the previous global survey offers numerous examples of a single poisoned arrow killing men, as well as big game animals, one not well read on the subject might question that a minute amount of poison could kill a man. The lethality of several poisoned arrows striking one man, however, is undeniable.

Experts note the presence of the gas-gangrene organism in snakes' mouths and snakebite wounds and confirm that this infection frequently kills when the venom itself does not. The medical literature defines a poisonous snakebite as a "contaminated venom-laden anaerobic puncture wound, which predisposes to infection and tissue destruction."[6] Indian arrow poisons were commonly left to rot prior to application.

Although many poisons from plant sources contain substances of undoubted pharmacological activity, most derived from animals probably exert their principal effect by inducing gas-gangrene, tetanus, and other severe infections. Spores of tetanus and gas-gangrene bacteria abound in decaying animal matter. Significantly, arrows treated with rapidly acting plant poisons are used only for hunting among many tribes whereas those tainted with animal toxins are relegated to war.[7]

Decomposition, or putrification, results when body defenses can no longer hold bacteria in check. In decaying organic matter, bacteria mass in quantity literally to digest the soft tissues of the body, ultimately reducing them to fluid and gas. The ability of arrow and lance poisons to kill elephants (Africa, India) and whales (Aleut Islands, Kodiak Islands) is understandable when one considers the ingredients being injected. The effects are often dramatic in the extreme. Victims of *Cicuta* poisoning can dislocate limbs, bite off their tongues, and crush their teeth while writhing from the pain. The description, cited earlier, of a cavalry horse struck by a Navaho poisoned arrow includes the observation that it swelled, while suffering great pain, and was dead the following morning. An army surgeon's recounting of a Lipan Apache poison-arrow victim noted that, though he sustained only a slight scratch, the victim's flesh sloughed away, exposing the ribs.

An Opata poisoned arrow nicked the hand of a member of Coronado's expedition, who was dead two days later. He was one of seventeen men Coronado lost while moving through Sonora. Pedro de Castaneda de Nagera, traveling with Coronado in 1540, chronicled a soldier struck by a poison arrow whose skin rotted and fell off, leaving the bones and sinews bare and producing a horrible odor.

Although the worldwide use of poisoned arrows and the resulting casualties and suffering are clearly documented, still Henrietta Stockel wrote in 1995, "The toxic effect of poisoned-tipped arrows has always been overplayed by Hollywood"[8] and "[t]he Indian's use of viscera from all types of animals as the poisoning agent is the stuff of legends."[9] The preceding compellingly challenges such an observation. Specifically, the Indians used "decomposed viscera" (as well as blood and pulped ants, bees, centipedes, spiders, and scorpions), which, in its ability to generate and host dangerous bacterial populations in the victim's body, is the real lethal threat.

Several tribes were cognizant of the infections brought on by their poisoned arrows, even though they did not understand the scientific basis. Their efforts were augmented by the fact that arrowheads, even those without poison, were frequently attached to the shaft so that the point could not be retrieved once it entered the body. Linda King has described this in detail: "Ethnographic evidence shows war arrows were designed to lodge the point in the wound. Frank Latta recorded for the Yokuts that the sinews attaching points to war arrows were not water-proofed; they were specially designed so that blood would loosen the sinews and allow the point to remain in the wound when the foreshaft was removed." [10]

Texas historian A. J. Sowell left this 1851 account of a Texas settler's reaction to a Comanche arrow wound: "Tom was wounded in the leg by an arrow, and when it was withdrawn the spike remained, but was not noticed at the time, as the man who pulled it out threw it down without looking at it. The wound would never heal, and two years after it was sore and running corruption." [11] Another document, six years earlier, reads, "When Kelso drew the arrow from his wound during the fight and threw it down, he failed to notice in the excitement of the time that the spike had failed to come with the shaft. For twenty-two years the wound would not heal until by a surgical operation the iron arrow head was discovered and removed, and the wound then healed." [12]

Finally, Stockel asserts that the Indians did not require arrow poison because "[they] were such skilled bowmen that any enhancement of the basics was normally unnecessary." [13] A deeper reading on the subject of North American Indian warfare and weaponry reveals that, at the time of cultural contact, Indians throughout North America and adjacent regions wore various types of armor, including helmets of thick wood and rawhide, and carried shields capable of deflecting musket balls. In fact, there is an almost 100 percent correlation between the wearing of armor and the presence of poisoned arrows. [14] Stockel's "skilled bowman" would be relatively helpless against an enemy adorned with multilayered rawhide cuirass, helmet, and shield; however, with poisoned arrows, a fighter had merely to inflict a scratch, which was much more likely than a deep penetration of rod, slat, or quilted multi-ply rawhide armor.

As for the question of when and why arrow poisoning arose in North America, the appearance and disappearance of weapons is often explained in terms of the offensive/defensive weapons spiral model: an offensive weapon advancement by side A is countered by a defensive weapon development by side B. The resulting stalemate exists until one side trumps the other's weaponry, which in turn kicks the offensive/defensive spiral into action once more. The hostilities continue until one side is stymied. Many factors determine military superiority, but response to an enemy's weapons system is obviously of paramount importance.

It is also true that weapons sometimes evolve without the necessity of an enemy. The muzzle-loading, smoothbore flintlock musket served as the standard weapon of Europeans after 1650. Modifications in the 1700s refined the basic weapon's muzzle velocity and accuracy, and in the mid-1880s developments led to the breech-loading rifle. Some repeating rifles were also in evidence. Clearly the nation with firearms of greater range and accuracy held a slight, or even great, advantage over an adversary who lagged in the spiral.

The bow and arrow likewise experienced an evolution that increased its range and impact. The Spanish recorded that the sinew-backed bows of the Southwestern Indians could penetrate their armor. Earlier these Indians had shot a simple self-bow, which could propel an arrow thirty-five meters per second, much superior to the earlier atlatl, or throwing-stick dart, which traveled at only twenty-one meters per second. The sinew-backed bow, however, could throw an arrow at forty-three meters per second.[15]

Although it would be impossible to prove definitively, poison arrows might have spurred the creation of more complex armor in Native North America. The potential lethality of a poisoned arrow is central in a discussion of its use: it need not instantly kill to be effective. An enemy's concentration and the tremendous hand-eye coordination essential to wield archaic weapons effectively would be unsettled by the sting, as well as the psychological terror of knowing that one had been struck by a poisoned projectile, thereby weakening him. An infected wound would remove a fighter from the martial roster.

The practice of projectile-point poisoning may have first appeared in the Paleo-Indian period and was certainly widespread at the time of contact. All major Native American cultures have been cited through ethnobotanical, ethnohistorical, or ethnographic sources as having knowledge of arrow-poison manufacture.

Appendix

North American Indian Tribes That Used Arrow Poison and Types of Poison Used

GROUP	POISON
Achumawi	Arrow poison use cited, but ingredients unknown
Acoma Pueblo	*Ranunculus spp.* (butter cup)
Alabama	*Eryngium virginianum* (bear grass)
Aleut	*Aconitum spp.*, rancid human fat (sometimes brains specified) and the crushed bodies of small poisonous worms found in freshwater lakes
Apache (general)	(A) Rattlesnake venom, crushed red ants, centipedes, and scorpions
	(B) Dried and powdered deer spleen mixed with roots or stalks of nettles, and an unidentified plant that had a burning taste "like chili." The mixture was placed in a bag made from a deer's big intestine, which was hung from a tree for three days until rotten and ready for use.
	(c) Unidentified species of lichen that grows on "heavy rocks," added to "B" poison
	(D) Made from unidentified insect
Blackfeet (Siksika, Kainah, Piegan)	Chewed the berries of *Cornus sericea* (red osier dogwood) and spit the juice on the points of their war arrows to cause infection
Cahuilla	Arrow poison use cited, but ingredients unknown
California Indians	(A) *Piperacea spp.* (American pepper plant), for general use
	(B) *Evernia spp.* (wolf moss)
	(c) *Eremocarpus setigerus* (turkey mullen)

Catawba	Arrow poison use cited, but ingredients unknown
Cherokee	A root was chewed and juice was applied to arrow; species unknown
Cheyenne	*Potentilla fruticosa* (shrubby cinquefoil)
Chickahominy	Liver infused with rattlesnake venom, mashed into thick paste, and applied to arrow point
Chiricahua Apache	Rotted animal blood and prickly pear cactus spines
Chumash	Arrow poison use cited, but ingredients unknown
Clallam	Copper arrow points soaked in seawater to corrode and thereby create a dangerous wound
Cree (Hudson Bay)	*Heracleum maximum* (cow parsnip)
Creek	"Some very poisonous and deadly substance"; ingredients unknown
Erie	Rattlesnake venom
Gabrielino	Arrow poison use cited, but ingredients unknown
Gosiute	*Erigeron gandiflorus* (large flower fleabane), *Valeriana dioica* (marsh valerian), *Valeriana sylvatica* (woods valerian). To this mixture, *Cicuta douglasii* was sometimes added.
Haisla	*Cicuta douglasii*
Hanaksiala	*Cicuta douglasii*
Havasupai	Infusion from boiled leaves of *Ptelea trifoliata* (common hop tree) and a "black substance" inside large scorpions, centipedes, and red ants. Matginyue (a small biting insect), *Datura spp.* (jimson weed), and *Quagamuna* (a weed that grows on sandy banks) were mixed, mashed, dried, and stored before being applied by wetting a small amount with the liquid wrung from heated soap weed leaves.
Hopi	Liver infused with rattlesnake venom, buried until rotted; paste was painted on arrow

	points, which were allowed to dry before being dipped in blood.
Hupa	Use of flint considered to be poisonous; also stone arrow points found in the vicinity of one of their ancient villages
Illini	Legendary mention of copperhead venom
Interior Salish	(A) Rattlensnake venom
	(B) Rattlesnake venom mixed with crushed flowers of *Ranunculus spp.*
Isleta Pueblo	*Chrysothamnus nauseosus* (rabbit bush), an infusion of which was applied to arrow foreshaft made from *Triplex canescens* (fourwing saltbush); this plant was used for poison arrows ("swift" or "war" arrows), because the fragile *Triplex* tended to break off inside the body of the victim; the Isleta people also considered *Triplex* poisonous and capable of causing infections.
Kaniagmiut Inuit	Pulverized root of *Aconitum spp.*, mixed with a little water and allowed to ferment before use
Karok	(A) *Toxicodendron diversilobum* (Pacific poison oak) used only in hunting
	(B) Rotted rattlesnake brains used for war arrows
Kawaiisu	Arrow poison use cited, but ingredients unknown
Koasati	*Eryngium virginianum* (bear grass)
Kodiaks	Mashed root of *Aconitum spp.*
Konkow	Arrow poison use cited, but ingredients unknown
Kwakiutl	*Cicuta douglasii*
Laguna Pueblo	"Snake venom and mud"
Lillooet	Rattlesnake venom
Lipan Apache	*Yucca angustifola*
Maidu	(A) Liver infused with rattlesnake venom; mixture left to rot prior to application

	(B) Arrow points imbedded in *Evernia spp.* (wolf moss) for as long as a year; rattlesnake venom sometimes added
Mattaponi	Rattlesnake venom glands mixed into a paste
Micmac	Herbal arrow poison cited; ingredients unknown
Modoc	Arrow poison use cited, but ingredients unknown
Mono	(A) Rotted deer liver dried in the sun and powdered prior to use
	(B) Liver infused with rattlesnake venom
Moqui	Liver infused with rattlesnake venom; mixture allowed to rot and coated with blood before application to points
Natchez	"Vine with long thin pods"; species unknown
Navaho	(A) Rattlesnake blood, juice of *Yucca spp.*; charcoal made from pith of *Yucca spp.*; resulting mixture applied to the point and about six inches up arrow shaft
	(B) Infusion of *Usnea barbarta* (alpine lichen) mixed with decayed animal liver and buried until rotten
	(C) *Rhus toxicodendron* (poison ivy), *Haceplia crenulat* (wild heliotrope) mixed with charcoal from a lightning-struck northern red oak
	(D) *Opuntia polyacantha* (plains pricklepear), *Yucca glauca* (small soapweed), and *Toxicodendron radicans* (eastern poison ivy)
	(E) Suspend dead rattlesnake over vessel into which putrid matter from decaying snake is collected; this is mixed with snake's venom and applied to arrow points.
Nez Perce	Rattlesnake venom
Nootka	*Veratrum viride*
North Carolina Indians	Arrow poison use cited, but ingredients unknown

Okanagan-Colville	(A) Arrow point coated with pulverized root of *Zigadenus venenosus* (death camus)
	(B) Roots of *Cicuta douglasii,* powdered and applied to arrow point prior to use
	(C) *Ranunculus glaberrimus* (sagebrush buttercup)
	(D) Decoction of mashed juniper (*Juniperus communis*) berries and branches
Omaha	Arrow poison use cited, but ingredients unknown
Oneida	Meat of poisonous blue otter
Opata	Arrow poison use cited, but ingredients unknown
Paiute	(A) *Akwasi,* "black-looking stuff on deer's intestines"; allowed to decay before use
	(B) *Cicuta spp.,* mashed, applied to arrow point, and allowed to dry
Pima	(A) *Euphorbia spp.,* mixed with pulp of prickly pear stem segments
	(B) Putrid meat
Pit River Indians	Dog's liver mixed with juice of wild parsnip
Plains Cree	Arrow poison use cited, but ingredients unknown
Pomo	"Magical" arrow poison made from rattlesnake blood, pulped spiders, bees, ants, and scorpions; applied to tip of arrow that was shot over an enemy's house
Powhatan	Rattlesnake venom glands mixed into a paste
Rappahannock	Beef liver mashed into pulp and packed tightly into an animal bladder; rattlesnake induced to strike bag, which was then buried until the contents putrefied and it was considered ready for use.
Seminole	Rattlesnake venom infused into liver; liver buried until putrefied and ready for use
Seneca	Arrow poison use cited, but ingredients unknown

Seri	*Marsdenia spp., Jatropha cinerea, J. cuneata, Euphorbia spp.,* and *Sapium biloculare*
Shoshone	(A) Rattlesnake venom
	(B) Rattlesnake venom mixed with crushed ants and mashed animal spleen; mixture allowed to decay before use
Sisseton Sioux	Mixed small spines of prickly pear cactus with grease and applied to arrow points
Stalo	Decayed human brains
Teton Sioux	Liver infused with rattlesnake venom and allowed to rot before use
Thompson Indians	(A) Rattlesnake venom and crushed flowers of *Ranunculus spp.*
	(B) *Artemisia dracunculus* (wormwood), *Cornus sericea, Ranunculus sceleratus* (celery leaf buttercup)
	(C) *R. sceleratus* rubbed on arrow before use
Tolowa	*Toxicodendron diversilobum* used only in hunting
Tonkawa	Juice of mistletoe applied to arrow point
Virginia Indians	Arrow poison use cited, but ingredients (roots) unknown
Western Apache	Human saliva, deer spleen, and nettles; mixture allowed to decay before use
Yana	Deer liver infused with rattlesnake venom; allowed to decay before use
Yaqui	Arrow poison use cited, but ingredients unknown
Yavapais	Pulverized mixture of rattlesnake venom, spiders, centipedes, a variety of long-winged bee, and walnut leaves; mixture left to rot before use
Yuki	*Equisetum telmateia* (giant horsetail fern)
Yurok	*Toxicodendron diversilobum,* used only in hunting

Notes

Introduction

1. The information contained in the overview of biochemical warfare was drawn from several sources: Jeffery K. Smart, *Textbook of Military Medicine: Medical Aspects of Chemical and Biological Warfare* (Aberdeen, Md.: U.S. Army Chemical and Biological Defense Command, Aberdeen Proving Ground, 1997); J. Paxman and R. Harris, *A Higher Form of Killing: The Secret Story of Chemical and Biological Warfare* (New York: Hill and Wang, 1982); Adrienne Mayor, *Greek Fire, Poison Arrows, and Scorpion Bombs: Biological and Chemical Warfare in the Ancient World* (New York: Overlook Duckworth Publications, 2003).

2. David E. Jones, *Native North American Armor, Shields, and Fortifications* (Austin: University of Texas Press, 2004).

3. D. E. Worcester, "The Weapons of American Indians," *New Mexico Historical Review,* vol. 20, no. 8 (1945), p. 237.

4. *Dictionary of Daily Life of Indians of the Americas* (Newport Beach, Calif.: Publishers Incorporated, 1981), vol. 2: 1071.

5. Edmund Carpenter and Royal B. Hassrick, "Some Notes on Arrow Poisoning among the Tribes of the Eastern Woodlands," *Proceedings of the Delaware County Institute of Science,* vol. 21 (1957), p. 45.

6. John Swanton, "Early History of the Creek Indians and Their Neighbors," *Bulletin of the Bureau of American Ethnology,* vol. 73 (1922), and Regina Flannery, "An Analysis of Coastal Algonquin Culture," *Catholic University of America, Anthropological Series,* no. 7 (1939).

7. J. H. Hill, "Notes on Arrow Wounds," *American Journal of the Medical Sciences* (1862), p. 368.

8. Robert Brown, "On the Vegetable Products Used by American Indians," *Transactions of the Botanical Society,* vol. 9 (Edinburgh: Machlachlan, Stewart, and Company, 1868), p. 387.

9. Henrietta H. Stockel, *The Lightning Stick: Arrows, Wounds, and Indian Legends* (Reno: University of Nevada Press, 1995), p. xiv.

10. Stockel, *Lightning Stick,* p. 16.

11. Stockel, *Lightning Stick,* p. 104.

12. See John C. DaCosata, cited in Stockel, *Lightning Stick,* p. 16;

and John Culley, "The California Indians: Their Medical Practices and Their Drugs," *Journal of the American Pharmaceutical Association,* vol. 25, no. 4 (1936), p. 336.

13. D. L. Olmsted, "Achumawi." In *Handbook of North American Indians,* vol. 8. William C. Sturtevant, ed. (Washington, D.C.: Smithsonian Institution, 1990), p. 455; Lowell J. Bean, "Gabrielino." In *Handbook of North American Indians,* vol. 8. William C. Sturtevant, ed. (Washington, D.C.: Smithsonian Institution, 1990), p. 346; John B. Romero, *The Botanical Lore of the California Indians* (New York: Vantage Press, 1954), p. 38.

14. John Clayton, cited in W. J. Hoffman, "Poisoned Arrows," *American Anthropologist,* vol. 4 (1891), pp. 67–71.

15. Morris Opler, *Chiricahua Apache Material Relating to Sorcery* (Washington, D.C.: Catholic University of America Press, 1944), pp. 67–71.

16. W. Vernon Kinielz, *The Indians of the Western Great Lakes, 1615–1760* (Ann Arbor: University of Michigan Press, 1940), p. 69.

17. Romero, *Botanical Lore,* p. 35.

18. William W. Warren, *History of the Ojibway People* (St. Paul: Minnesota Historical Society, 1984).

Chapter One: On Plant Poisons

1. Edward R. Ricciuti, *The Devil's Garden: Facts and Folklore of Perilous Plants* (New York: Walker and Company, 1978), p. 61.

2. Ricciuti, *Devil's Garden,* p. 62.

3. Ricciuti, *Devil's Garden,* p. 64.

4. Henry M. Parrish, *Poisonous Snakebites in the United States* (New York: Vantage Press, 1980), p. 388.

5. Sherman A. Minton and Madge Rutherford Minton, *Venomous Reptiles* (New York: Charles Scribner's Sons, 1969), p. 121.

6. Ricciuti, *Devil's Garden,* p. 135.

7. Robert Beverly, quoted in Charles F. Saunders, *Edible and Useful Wild Plants of the United States and Canada* (New York: Dover, 1920), p. 249.

8. Ricciuti, *Devil's Garden,* p. 96.

Chapter Two: Nonmilitary Poisons

1. Father Sagard and W. N. Fenton [1630], "An Early Cherokee Ethnobotanical Note," *Journal of the Washington Academy of Science,* vol. 37. no. 3 (1947), p. 74.

2. Frederick Pursh, *Botanical Excursion in the Northeastern Parts of the*

States of Pennsylvania and New York during the Year 1807 (Onondaga, N.Y.: Onondaga Historical Association, 1868), p. 195.

3. James Herrick, *Iroquois Medical Botany* (Syracuse, N.Y.: Syracuse University Press, 1995), p. 195.

4. Regina Flannery, "An Analysis of Coastal Algonquin Culture," *Catholic University of America Anthropological Series,* no. 7 (1939), p. 133.

5. Flannery, "Coastal Algonquin Culture," p. 133.

6. Paul B. Hamel and Mary U. Chiltoskey, *Cherokee Plants and Their Uses: A 400-Year History* (Sylva, N.C.: Herald Publishing, 1972), p. 31.

7. J. W. Blankinship, "Native Economic Plants of Montana," *Montana Agricultural College Experimental Station Bulletin,* no. 56 (1905), p. 10.

8. Christine A. Heller, *Edible and Poisonous Plants of Alaska* (College, Alaska: Cooperative Extension Service in Agriculture and Home Economics, 1953), p. 153.

9. Daniel E. Moerman, *Native American Ethnobotany* (Portland, Ore.: Timber Press, 1998), p. 256. Moerman's work forms the basis for any work in specific areas of Native North American ethnobotany.

10. Moerman, *Native American Ethnobotany,* pp. 589–90.

11. Charles C. Jones, *Antiquities of the Southern Indians, Particularly of the Georgia Tribes* (Tuscaloosa: University of Alabama Press, 1999), p. 333.

12. V. K. Chestnut, *Plants Used by Indians of Mendocino Country, California* (Willitis, Calif.: Mendocino County Historical Society, 1974), p. 321.

13. Chestnut, *Indians of Mendocino County,* p. 321.

14. John B. Romero, *The Botanical Lore of the California Indians* (New York: Vantage Press, 1954), p. 62.

15. *Dictionary of Daily Life of Indians of the Americas.* 1981 Publishers Incorporated: Newport Beach, California. Vol. 2, p. 495.

16. Chestnut, *Indians of Mendocino County,* p. 285.

17. Edith V. A. Murphey, *Indian Uses of Native Plants* (Glenwood, Ill.: Myerbooks, 1958), p. 20.

18. Maurice L. Zigmond, *Kawaiisu Ethnobotany* (Salt Lake City: University of Utah Press, 1981), p. 64.

19. John Culley, "The California Indians: Their Medical Practices and Their Drugs," *Journal of the American Pharmaceutical Association,* vol. 25, no. 4 (1936), p. 336.

20. Nancy J. Turner, *Food Plants of Interior First Peoples* (Vancouver: University of British Columbia Press, 1997), p. 83. Turner and her colleagues are at the center of ethnobotanical investigation of the Northwest Coast.

21. James Michael Mahar, "Ethnobotany of the Oregon Paiutes of the Warm Springs Indian Reservation," Ph.D. dissertation, Reed College, 1953, p. 87.

22. Frederick Webb Hodge, *Handbook of American Indians North of Mexico.* Part 2. Smithsonian Institution, Bureau of American Ethnology, Bulletin 30 (Washington, D.C.: Government Printing Office), p. 273.

23. Hamel and Chiltoskey, *Cherokee Plants,* p. 55.

24. Moerman, *Native American Ethnobotany,* p. 424.

25. J. Witthoft, "An Early Cherokee Ethnobotanical Note," *Washington Academy of Sciences,* vol. 37 (1954), pp. 73–75.

26. Gladys Tantaquidgeon, "Folk Medicine of The Delaware and Related Algonquian Indians," *Pennsylvania Historical Museum Commission Anthropological Series,* no. 3 (1972), p. 3.

27. Carolyn Keller Reeves, *The Choctaw before Removal* (Jackson: University Press of Mississippi, 1985), p. 49.

28. J. Sharpe and T. B. Underwood, *American Indian Cooking and Herb Lore* (Cherokee, N.C.: Cherokee Publications, 1973), p. 32.

29. Michael A. Weiner, *Earth Medicines—Earth Foods* (New York: Collier Books, 1972), p. 76.

30. Weiner, *Earth Medicines,* p. 76.

31. Richard S. Felger and Mary Beck Moser, *People of the Desert and Sea* (Tucson: University of Arizona Press, 1985), p. 243.

32. Moerman, *Native American Ethnobotany,* p. 625.

33. Robert F. Heizer, "Aconite Poison Whaling in Asia and America: An Aleutian Transfer to the New World," *Smithsonian Institution, Bureau of American Ethnology Bulletin,* vol. 133, no. 24 (1938), p. 437.

34. Martin Sauer, *An Account of A Geographical and Astronomical Expedition to the North Parts of Russian Performed by Commodore Joseph Billings: 1785–1794* (London: A. Strahan, 1802), p. 177.

35. Marc Andre Baker, "The Ethnobotany of the Yurok, Tolowa, and Karok Indians of Northwestern California," master's thesis, Humboldt State University, p. 117.

36. Moerman, *Native American Ethnobotany,* p. 178.

37. S. Powers, "Aboriginal Botany," *Proceedings of the California Academy of Science,* vol. 5 (1873), p. 375.

38. John Brickell, *The Natural History of North Carolina* (New York: Johnson Reprint Corporation, [1737] 1969).

39. Virgil J. Vogel, *American Indian Medicine* (Norman: University of Oklahoma Press, 1949), p. 166.

40. John Swanton, "Aboriginal Culture of the Southeast," *Forty-Second Annual Report of the Bureau of American Ethnology to the Secretary of*

the Smithsonian Institution (Washington, D.C.: Smithsonian Institution, 1924), p. 714.

41. Moerman, *Native American Ethnobotany*, p. 91.

42. Moerman, *Native American Ethnobotany*, p. 131.

43. Herrick, *Iroquois Medical Botany*, p. 195.

44. Herrick, *Iroquois Medical Botany*, p. 450.

45. Herrick, *Iroquois Medical Botany*, p. 457.

46. Moerman, *Native American Ethnobotany*, p. 137.

47. Meredith J. Black, *Algonquin Ethnobotany: An Interpretation of Aboriginal Adaptations in Southwestern Quebec*, Canadian Ethnology Service Papers no. 65 (Ottawa: National Museum of Canada, 1980), p. 206.

48. Huron H. Smith, "Ethnobotany of the Menomini Indians," *Bulletin of the Public Museum of the City of Milwaukee*, vol. 4, no. 1 (1923), pp. 1-75.

49. Huron H. Smith, "Ethnobotany of the Ojibwe Indians," *Bulletin of the Public Museum of the City of Milwaukee*, vol. 4, no. 3 (1922), pp. 327-525.

50. Moerman, *Native American Ethnobotany*, p. 397.

51. Frances Densmore, "Uses of Plants by the Chippewa Indians." *Forty-Fourth Annual Report of the Bureau of American Ethnology to the Secretary of the Smithsonian Institution* (Washington, D.C.: Smithsonian Institution, 1926), pp. 275-305.

52. Vogel, *American Indian Medicine*, 167.

53. Frank G. Speck, "Catawba Herbal and Curative Practices," *Journal of American Folklore*, vol. 57 (1937), pp. 45-47.

54. Moerman, *Native American Ethnobotany*, p. 613.

55. M. R. Gilmore, "Uses of Plants by the Indians of the Missouri River Region," *Thirty-Third Annual Report of the Bureau of American Ethnology* (Washington, D.C.: Smithsonian Institution, 1919), pp. 43-54.

56. Gilmore "Uses of Plants," p. 99.

57. Moerman, *Native American Ethnobotany*, p. 385.

58. W. E. Safford, "Narcotic Plants and Stimulants of the Ancient Americas," *Annual Report of the Smithsonian Institution* (Washington, D.C.: Smithsonian Institution, 1916), p. 397.

59. Mahar, "Ethnobotany of the Oregon Paiutes," p. 54.

60. Moerman, *Native American Ethnobotany*, p. 613.

61. Moerman, *Native American Ethnobotany*, p. 219.

62. Moerman, *Native American Ethnobotany*, p. 46.

63. Turner, *Food Plants of Interior First Peoples*, p. 182.

64. Moerman, *Native American Ethnobotany*, p. 589.

65. Moerman, *Native American Ethnobotany*, p. 568.

66. Moerman, *Native American Ethnobotany,* p. 319.

67. Moerman, *Native American Ethnobotany,* p. 173.

68. Jennie Goodrich, *Kashaya Pomo Plants* (Los Angeles: American Indian Studies Center, University of California, Los Angeles), p. 128.

69. Moerman, *Native American Ethnobotany,* p. 590.

70. Jan Timbrook, "Ethnobotany of the Chumash Indians. California. Based on Collections by John P. Harrington," *Economic Botany,* vol. 44, no. 2 (1990), p. 246.

71. Paul A. Vestal, "Ethnobotany of the Ramah Navaho." *Papers of the Peabody Museum of American Archaeology and Ethnology: Howard University,* vol. 60, no. 4 (1944), p. 16.

72. Frances H. Elmore, *Ethnobotany of the Navaho* (Albuquerque: University of New Mexico Press, 1944), p. 59.

73. Moerman, *Native American Ethnobotany,* p. 336.

74. Nancy J. Turner, "The Ethnobotany of the Bella Coola Indians of British Columbia," *Syesis: Provincial Museum of British Columbia,* vol. 6 (1973), pp. 193–220.

75. Turner, "Ethnobotany of the Bella Coola Indians," p. 208.

76. Brian D. Compton, "Upper North Wakashan and Southern Tsimshian Ethnobotany: The Knowledge and Usage of Plants and Fungi among the Oweekeno, Hanaksiala, Haisla, and Kitasoo Peoples of the Central and North Coasts of British Columbia," Ph.D. dissertation, University of British Columbia, 1993, p. 217.

77. Compton, "Upper North Wakashan and Southern Tsimshian Ethnobotany," p. 202.

78. Moerman, *Native American Ethnobotany,* p. 371.

79. Moerman, *Native American Ethnobotany,* p. 173.

80. Moerman, *Native American Ethnobotany,* p. 590.

81. Heller, *Edible and Poisonous Plants of Alaska,* p. 163.

82. Heller, *Edible and Poisonous Plants of Alaska,* p. 159.

83. Moerman, *Native American Ethnobotany,* p. 468.

84. Alex Johnston, "Plants and The Blackfoot," *Lethbridge Historical Society: Occasional Papers,* no. 15 (1987), p. 35.

85. Weiner, *Earth Medicines,* p. 77.

86. Sandra Leslie Peacock, "Piikani Ethnobotany: The Traditional Plant Knowledge of the Piikani Peoples of the Northwestern Plains," master's thesis, University of Calgary, 1968.

87. Patrick Munson, "Contributions to Osage and Lakota Ethnobotany," *Plains Anthropologist,* vol. 26 (1981), p. 235.

88. Munson, "Osage and Lakota Ethnobotany," p. 238.

89. Herbert W. Kuhm, "Uses of Native Herbs by Wisconsin Indians," *Wisconsin Archaeologist,* vol. 42, no. 3 (1961), p. 114.

90. James A. Duke, *Handbook of Northeastern Indian Medicinal Plants* (Lincoln, Mass.: Quarterman Publications, 1986), p. 76.

91. Weiner, *Earth Medicines,* p.65.

92. Robin J. Marles and J. Christina Clavelle, *Aboriginal Plant Use in Canada's Northwest Boreal Forests* (Vancouver: University of British Columbia Press, 2000), p. 48.

93. Marles and Clavelle, *Aboriginal Plant Use,* p. 51.

94. Duke, *Handbook,* p. 68.

95. Roy Johnson, *The Tuscaroras* (Murfreesboro, N.C.: Johnson Publishing, 1967), p. 198.

96. Duke, *Handbook,* p. 74.

97. Duke, *Handbook,* p. 167.

98. Hamel and Chiltoskey, *Cherokee Plants and Their Uses,* p. 31.

99. William H. Banks, "Ethnobotany of the Cherokee Indians," master's thesis, University of Tennessee, 1953, p. 48.

100. Weiner, *Earth Medicines,* p. 65.

101. W. N. Fenton, "An Early Cherokee Ethnobotanical Note," *Journal of the Washington Academy of Science,* vol. 37, no. 3 (1947), p. 74.

102. Weiner, *Earth Medicines,* p. 77.

103. Sandra S. Strike, *Ethnobotany of the California Indians.* Vol. 2: *Aboriginal Uses of California's Indigenous Plants* (Königstein, Germany: Koeltz Scientific, 1994), p. 9.

104. Robert H. Heizer and Albert B. Elsasser, *The Natural World of the California Indians* (Los Angeles: University of California Press, 1980), p. 248.

105. Strike, *Ethnobotany of the California Indians,* p. 16.

106. Strike, *Ethnobotany of the California Indians,* p. 51.

107. Strike, *Ethnobotany of the California Indians,* p. 57.

108. Strike, *Ethnobotany of the California Indians,* p. 61.

109. Barbara R. Bocek, "Ethnobotany of Costanoan Indians, California. Based on Collections by John P. Harrington." *Economic Botany,* vol. 38, no. 2 (1967), p. 249.

110. Strike, *Ethnobotany of the California Indians,* p. 101.

111. Strike, *Ethnobotany of the California Indians,* p. 101.

112. Strike, *Ethnobotany of the California Indians,* p. 149.

113. Timbrook, "Ethnobotany of the Chumash Indians," p. 253.

114. Nancy J. Turner, *Food Plants of Coastal First Peoples* (Vancouver: University of British Columbia Press, 1995), p. 11.

115. Kathleen Lynch, *Dena'ina K'etuna: Taniana Plantlore* (Anchorage, Alaska: Adult Literacy Laboratory. Anchorage Community College, 1977), p. 36.

Chapter Three: World Survey of Arrow Poisoning

1. Edward R. Ricciuti, The Devil's Garden: Facts and Folklore of Perilous Plants (New York: Walker and Company, 1978), p. 123.

2. Adrienne Mayor, "Dirty Tricks in Ancient Warfare," Quarterly Journal of Military History, vol. 30, no. 2 (1997), p. 36.

3. W. J. Hoffman, "Poisoned Arrows." American Anthropologist, vol. 4 (1891), p. 67.

4. Edmund Burke, The History of Archery (New York: William Morrow, 1957), p. 69.

5. D. R. Feng and L. G. Kilborn, "Nosu and Miao Arrow Poisons," Journal of the West China Border Research Society, vol. 9 (1937), p. 132.

6. Hoffman, "Poisoned Arrows," p. 167.

7. Burke, History of Archery, p. 78.

8. S. Eldridge, "On the Arrow Poisons in Use among Ainos of Yeo," Transactions of the Asiatic Society, vol. 4 (1897), p. 78; John Batchelor, The Ainu of Japan (London: Religious Tract Society, 1892); C. J. Longman and W. Walrond, Archery (London: Longman, Green, 1894).

9. Batchelor, The Ainu, p. 169.

10. Longman and Walrond, Archery, p. 96.

11. J. U. Lloyd and C. G. Lloyd, Drugs and Medicines of North America (Cincinnati: J. U. Lloyd and C. G. Lloyd, 1884), p. 23.

12. Robert F. Heizer, "Aconite Arrow Poison in the Old and New World," Journal of the Washington Academy of Sciences, vol. 28 (1938), pp. 358–64.

13. Torao Mozai, "Kublai Khan's Lost Fleet," National Geographic, vol. 162, no. 5 (1982), p. 634.

14. Eldridge, "Arrow Poisons in Use among Ainos," p. 81.

15. Edouard Chavannes, trans., Les memoires historiques de Se-ma Ts'ien (Paris: Maisconneuve, 1906), p. 226.

16. Feng and Kilborn, "Nosu and Miao Arrow Poisons," pp. 130–132.

17. http://www.atarn/Chinese/yn-bow.htm.

18. Feng and Kilborn, "Nosu and Miao Arrow Poisons," p. 134.

19. Heizer, "Aconite Arrow Poison in the Old and New World," p. 363.

20. Frances Hamilton, "An Account of a Genus including the Herba Toxicaria of the Himalayan Mountains; Or, the Plant with Which the Natives Poison Their Arrows." Edinburgh Journal of Science, vol. 2 (1824), p. 25.

21. Eldridge, "Arrow Poisons in Use among Ainos," p. 7.

22. Eldridge, "Arrow Poisons in Use among Ainos," p. 80.

23. Thomas R. Fraser, "The Poisoned Arrows of the Abors and Mishmis of North-Eastern India and the Composition and Action of Their Poisons." *Transactions of the Royal Society of Edinburgh,* vol. 50 (1916), p. 897.

24. Fraser, "Poisoned Arrows of the Abors and Mishmis," p. 898.

25. Fraser, "Poisoned Arrows of the Abors and Mishmis," p. 901.

26. Fraser, "Poisoned Arrows of the Abors and Mishmis," p. 920.

27. Fraser, "Poisoned Arrows of the Abors and Mishmis," p. 928.

28. Fraser, "Poisoned Arrows of the Abors and Mishmis," p. 926.

29. Sherman A. Minton and Madge Rutherford Minton, *Venomous Reptiles* (New York: Charles Scribner's Sons, 1969), p. 121.

30. Longman and Walrond, *Archery,* p. 101.

31. Carleton S. Coon, *The Hunting People* (Boston: Little, Brown, 1970), p. 81.

32. Alan Burns, *History of Nigeria* (London: George Allen and Unwin, 1969), p. 60.

33. R. C. Abraham, *The Tiv Peoples* (Lagos: Government Printer, 1933), p. 91.

34. Christopher Spring, *African Arms and Armor* (Washington, D.C.: Smithsonian Institution Press, 1993), p. 45.

35. "Poison Used on Zulu Arrows Found to Fight Cancerous Tumors" [http://www.jcrows.com/zulu.html]

36. Ricciuti, *Devil's Garden,* p. 122.

37. Spring, *African Arms and Armor,* p. 52.

38. James A. Horton, *West African Countries and Peoples* (Edinburgh: University Press, 1868), p. 147.

39. H. Ling Roth, *Great Benin: Its Customs, Arts, and Horrors* (New York: Barnes and Noble, 1966), p. 46.

40. "Entry by Troops Revelation Chapter" [http://www.entryby troops.org/Revelation/chapter9.hym].

41. Eldridge, "Arrow Poisons in Use among Ainos," pp. 78–79.

42. Hoffman, "Poisoned Arrows," p. 68.

43. Ricciuti, *Devil's Garden,* p. 122.

44. Heizer, "Aconite Arrow Poison in the Old and New World," p. 443.

45. Daniel F. Austin, "Historically Important Plants of Southeastern Florida," *Florida Anthropologist,* vol. 33, no. 1 (1980), p. 4.

46. Virgil J. Vogel, *American Indian Medicine* (Norman: University of Oklahoma Press, 1949), p. 393.

47. Hoffman, "Poisoned Arrows," p. 68.

48. Longman and Walrond, *Archery,* p. 103.

49. Ricciuti, *Devil's Garden,* p. 119.

50. Emmett F. Gibson, "Filipinos Blast Jap Chutists," *Chicago Herald-American,* July 1942.

51. Ricciuti, *Devil's Garden,* p. 122.

52. M. Cox Balick, *Plants, People, and Culture: The Science of Ethnobotany* (New York: Scientific American Library, 1996), p. 35.

Chapter Four: Arrow Poisons of the North American Indians

1. Edmund Carpenter and Royal B. Hassrick, "Some Notes on Arrow Poisoning among the Tribes of the Eastern Woodlands," *Proceedings of the Delaware County Institute of Science,* vol. 10, no. 2 (1957), p. 52.

2. David Cusick, *Ancient History of the Six Nations* (Lockport, N.Y.: Turner and McCollum, 1848), p. 33.

3. H. M. Converse, "Myths and Legends of the Iroquois," *New York State Museum Bulletin,* no. 125 (1908), p. 55.

4. Wilson D. Wallis and Ruth Sawtell Wallis, *The Micmac Indians of Eastern Canada* (Minneapolis: University of Minnesota Press, 1952), p. 33.

5. Carpenter and Hassrick, "Notes on Arrow Poisoning," p. 47.

6. John Brickell, *The Natural History of North Carolina* (New York: Johnson Reprint Corporation, [1737] 1969), p. 394.

7. Carpenter and Hassrick, "Notes on Arrow Poisoning," p. 50.

8. Carpenter and Hassrick, "Notes on Arrow Poisoning," p. 50.

9. Frank G. Speck, "Chapters on the Ethnology of the Powhatan Tribes of Virginia," *Museum of the American Indian, Heye Foundation: Indian Notes,* vol. 1, no. 5 (1928), p. 350.

10. Carpenter and Hassrick, "Notes on Arrow Poisoning," p. 51.

11. Carpenter and Hassrick, "Notes on Arrow Poisoning," p. 46.

12. Carpenter and Hassrick, "Notes on Arrow Poisoning," p. 47.

13. James Smith, *An Account of the Remarkable Occurrences in the Life and Travels of Colonel James Smith* (Cincinnati: Robert Clarke and Co., 1868), p. 21.

14. Carpenter and Hassrick, "Notes on Arrow Poisoning," p. 47.

15. Lyda Averill Taylor, *Plants Used as Curatives by Certain Southeastern Tribes* (Cambridge, Mass.: Botanical Museum of Harvard University, 1940), p. 67.

16. Francis H. Elmore, *Ethnobotany of the Navaho* (Albuquerque: University of New Mexico Press, 1944), p. 65.

17. Leland Wyman and Stuart K. Harris, "The Ethnobotany of the

Kayenta Navaho," *University of New Mexico Publications in Biology*, no. 5 (1951), p. 20.

18. Wyman and Harris, "Ethnobotany of the Kayenta Navaho," p. 70.

19. W. W. Hill, "Navaho Warfare." *Yale University Publications in Anthropology*, no. 5, p. 10.

20. Daniel E. Moerman, *Native American Ethnobotany* (Portland, Ore.: Timber Press, 1998), p. 367.

21. Elmore, *Ethnobotany of the Navaho*, p. 96.

22. "Sacred Hopi Texts" [http://www.sacred-texts.com/nam/hopi/toth/thoh−108.hym]

23. W. J. Hoffman, "Poisoned Arrows," *American Anthropologist*, vol. 4 (1891), p. 69.

24. Keith H. Basso, ed., *Western Apache Raiding and Warfare (From the Notes of Grenville Goodwin)* (Tucson: University of Arizona Press, 1971), pp. 231−32.

25. Basso, *Western Apache Raiding and Warfare*, p. 232.

26. Basso, *Western Apache Raiding and Warfare*, p. 232.

27. Basso, *Western Apache Raiding and Warfare*, p. 233.

28. Henrietta H. Stockel, *The Lightning Stick: Arrows, Wounds, and Indian Legends* (Reno: University of Nevada Press, 1995), p. 54.

29. Moerman, *Native American Ethnobotany*, p. 161.

30. Moerman, *Native American Ethnobotany*, p. 469.

31. Pedro Castaneda, *The Journey of Coronado* (Ann Arbor, Mich.: University Microfilms, 1966), p. 60.

32. C. Hanson, "The Deadly Arrow." *Museum of the Fur Trade Quarterly*, vol. 3, no. 4 (1967), p. 4.

33. J. B. Hill, "Notes on Arrow Wounds," *American Journal of the Medical Sciences* (1862), p. 368.

34. Moerman, *Native American Ethnobotany*, p. 452.

35. Leslie Spier, "Havasupai Ethnography." *Anthropological Papers of the American Museum of Natural History*, vol. 29, pt. 3, p. 249.

36. David M. Brugge, "History, Huki, and Warfare: Some Random Data on The Lower Pima," *The Kiva*, vol. 26, no. 4 (1961), p. 13.

37. D. E. Worcester, "The Weapons of American Indians," *New Mexico Historical Review*, vol. 20, no. 8 (1945), p. 229.

38. Carpenter and Hassrick, "Notes on Arrow Poisoning," p. 46.

39. Marie Lucille Rocca-Arvay, "Assimilation and Resistance of the Yaqui Indians of Northern Mexico during the Colonial Period," Ph.D. dissertation, Columbia University, 1981, p. 101.

40. Richard S. Felger and Mark Beck Moser, *People of the Desert and Sea* (Tucson: University of Arizona Press, 1985), p. 128.

41. Clifton B. Kroeber and Bernard L. Fontana, *Massacre on the Gila: An Account of the Last Major Battle between American Indians with Reflections on the Origin of War* (Tucson: University of Arizona Press, 1986), p. 73.

42. Winfred Buskirk, *The Western Apache* (Norman: University of Oklahoma Press, 1986), pp. 124–25.

43. Lowell J. Bean, "Gabrielino," in *Handbook of North American Indians*, vol. 8, William C. Sturtevant, ed. (Washington, D.C.: Smithsonian Institution, 1990), p. 544.

44. Lowell J. Bean and Katherine S. Saubel, *Temalpakh: Cahuilla Indian Knowledge and Usage of Plants* (Banning, Calif.: Malki Museum Press, 1972), p. 36.

45. Linda Barbey King, "Medea Creek Cemetery: Late Inland Chumash Patterns of Social Organization, Exchange and Warfare," Ph.D. dissertation, University of California, Los Angeles, 1982, p. 166.

46. Sherman A. Minton and Madge Rutherford Minton, *Venomous Reptiles* (New York: Charles Scribner's Sons, 1969), p. 168.

47. Maurice L. Zigmond, *Kawaiisu Ethnobotany* (Salt Lake City: University of Utah Press, 1981), p.67.

48. Ralph L. Beals, "Ethnology of the Nisenan," *University of California Publications in American Archaeology and Ethnology*, vol. 1 (1934), p. 341.

49. Carleton S. Coon, *The Hunting Peoples* (Boston: Little, Brown, 1970), p. 80.

50. Sandra S. Strike, *Ethnobotany of the California Indians*. Vol. 2: *Aboriginal Uses of California's Indigenous Plants* (Königstein, Germany: Koeltz Scientific Books, 1994), p. 62.

51. Marc Andre Baker, 1981 "The Ethnobotany of The Yurok, Tolowa, and Karok Indians of Northwestern California," master's thesis, Humboldt State University, 1981, p. 117.

52. Carl Meyer, 1971 "The Yurok of Trinidad Bay, 1851," in *The California Indians: A Source Book*, R. F. Heizer and M. A. Whipple, eds. (Berkeley: University of California Press, 1971), p. 203.

53. Sara M. Schenck and E. W. Gifford, 1952 "Karok Ethnobotany," *Anthropological Records*, vol. 13, no. 6 (1952), p. 384.

54. William J. Wallace, 1949 "Hupa Warfare." *Masterkey*, vol. 23 (1949), p. 71.

55. Pliny Earle Goddard, "Life and Culture of the Hupa," *University of California Publications in American Archaeology and Ethnology*, vol. 1, no. 1 (1903), p. 62.

56. L. S. Curtin, 1952 "Some Plants Used by the Yuki Indians of Round Valley, Northern California," *Southwest Museum Leaflets*, no. 27. (1952), p. 18.

57. D. L. Olmsted and Omer C. Stewart, "Achumawi," in *Handbook of North American Indians,* vol. 8, William C. Sturtevant, ed. (Washington, D.C.: Smithsonian Institution, 1990), p. 456.

58. Theodore Stern, 1990 "Klamath and Modoc," in *Handbook of North American Indians,* vol. 12, William C. Sturtevant, ed. (Washington, D.C.: Smithsonian Institution, 1990), p. 348.

59. John Bruno Romero, *The Botanical Lore of the California Indians* (New York: Vantage Press, 1954), p. 34.

60. Robert F. Heizer and Albert B. Elsasser, *The Natural World of the California Indians* (Los Angeles: University of California Press, 1980), p. 245.

61. Hoffman, "Poisoned Arrows," p. 70.

62. Strike, *Ethnobotany of the California Indians,* p. 58.

63. E. W. Gifford, "The Southern Yavapai," *University of California Publications in American Archaeology and Ethnology,* vol. 29 (1930), p. 64.

64. E. W. Gifford, "Atsugewi Ethnology," *University of California Publications, Anthropological Records,* vol. 14 (1950), p. 156.

65. Heizer and Elsasser, *Natural World of the California Indians,* p. 245.

66. Robert H. Lowie, "The Northern Shoshone," *Anthropological Papers of the American Museum of Natural History,* vol. 3, pt. 2 (1909), p. 192.

67. Erminie W. Voegelin, "Tubatulabal Ethnography," *University of California Anthropological Records,* vol. 2, no. 1 (1938), p. 28.

68. Moerman, *Native American Ethnobotany,* p. 587.

69. Moerman, *Native American Ethnobotany,* p. 355.

70. Moerman, *Native American Ethnobotany,* p. 468.

71. Ralph V. Chamberlin, "The Ethnobotany of the Gosiute Indians of Utah," *Papers of the American Anthropological Association,* pt. 5 (1974), p. 384.

72. Isabel T. Kelly, "Ethnobotany of the Surprise Valley Paiute," *University of California Publications in American Archaeology and Ethnology,* vol. 31 (1934), p. 145.

73. Kelly, "Ethnobotany of the Surprise Valley Paiute," p. 45.

74. Kelly, "Ethnobotany of the Surprise Valley Paiute," p. 145.

75. *Dictionary of Daily Life of the Indians of the Americas* (Newport Beach, Calif.: Publishers Incorporated, 1981), vol. 2: 141.

76. James Teit, "The Lillooet Indians," *Memoir of the American Museum of Natural History*, vol. 3 (1900), p. 263.

77. Moerman, *Native American Ethnobotany*, p. 178.

78. John B. Leiberg, "General Report on a Botanical Survey of the Coeur D'Alene Mountains in Idaho during the Summer of 1895," *U.S. Department of Agriculture: Divisions of Botany.* Vol. 5, no. 1 (1897), p. 101.

79. Nancy J. Turner, "Ethnobotany of the Okanagan-Colville Indians of British Columbia and Washington," *Occasional Papers of the British Columbia Provincial Museum*, no. 21 (1980), p. 50.

80. Moerman, *Native American Ethnobotany*, p. 164.

81. Turner, "Ethnobotany of the Okanagan-Colville Indians," p. 20.

82. Teit, "The Lillooet Indians," p. 235.

83. Moerman, *Native American Ethnobotany*, p. 179.

84. Hoffman, "Poisoned Arrows," p. 69.

85. Hoffman, "Poisoned Arrows," p. 70.

86. Jeffrey Hart, "The Ethnobotany of the Northern Cheyenne," *Journal of Ethnopharmacology*, vol. 4 (1981), p. 74.

87. Alice C. Fletcher and Francis L. Flesche, *The Omaha Tribe*, (Lincoln: University of Nebraska Press, 1972), 2:561.

88. David G. Mandelbaum, *The Plains Cree: An Ethnographical, Historical, and Comparative Study* (Regina, Saskatchewan: Canadian Research Center, University of Regina, 1979), p. 95.

89. W. W. Newcomb, *The Indians of Texas* (Austin: University of Texas Press, 1974), p. 140.

90. James Teit, "The Thompson Indians of British Columbia," *Memoir of the American Museum of Natural History*, vol. 2 (1900), p. 23.

91. Teit, "The Thompson Indians of British Columbia," p. 523.

92. Hoffman, "Poisoned Arrows," p. 162.

93. Moerman, *Native American Ethnobotany*, p. 162.

94. Turner, "Ethnobotany of the Okanagan-Colville Indians," p. 139.

95. Wilson Duff, "The Upper Stalo Indians of the Fraser Valley, British Columbia," *Anthropology in British Columbia, Memoir*, no. 1 (1952), p. 59.

96. Brian D. Compton, "Upper North Wakashan and Southern Tsimshian Ethnobotany: The Knowledge and Usage of Plants and Fungi among the Oweekeno, Hanaksiala, Haisla, and Kitasoo Peoples of the Central and North Coasts of British Columbia," Ph.D. dissertation, University of British Columbia, p. 203.

97. A. E. Porsild, "Edible Plants of the Arctic," *Calgary Arctic Institute of North America,* vol. 6 (1953), p. 17.

98. Diamond A. Jenness, "Algonquin Ethnobotany: An Interpretation of Aboriginal Adaptation in Southwestern Quebec," Canadian Ethnology Service, paper no. 65 (1980), p. 210.

99. Martin Sauer, *An Account of a Geographical and Astronomical Expedition to the North Parts of Russia Performed by Commodore Joseph Billings* (London: A. Strahan, 1802), p. 177.

100. J. B. Townsend, "Firearms against Native Arms," *Arctic Anthropology,* vol. 20, no. 2 (1983), p 23.

101. Townsend, "Firearms against Native Arms," p. 106.

102. Jenness, "Algonquin Ethnobotany," p. 210.

Chapter Five: Other Uses of Poisons in Warfare

1. John G. Bourke, "Remarks on Arrows and Arrow Makers," *American Anthropologist,* vol. 4, no. 1 (1891), p. 17.

2. W. W. Newcomb, *The Indians of Texas* (Austin: University of Texas Press, 1974), p. 140.

3. W. J. Hoffman, "Poisoned Arrows," *American Anthropologist,* vol. 4 (1891), p. 69.

4. Daniel E. Moerman, *Native American Ethnobotany* (Portland, Ore.: Timber Press, 1998), p. 179.

5. Diamond A. Jenness, "Algonquin Ethnobotany: An Interpretation of Aboriginal Adaptation in Southwestern Quebec," Canadian Ethnology Service, paper no. 65 (1980), p. 210.

6. Nancy J. Turner, "Ethnobotany of The Okanagan-Colville Indians of British Columbia and Washington," *Occasional Papers of the British Columbia Provincial Museum,* no. 21 (1980), p. 20.

7. Keith H. Basso, ed., *Western Apache Raiding and Warfare (From the Notes of Grenville Goodwin)* (Tucson: University of Arizona Press, 1971), p. 232.

8. Nancy J. Turner, "Ethnobotany of the Nitinaht Indians of Vancouver Island," *British Columbia Provincial Museum,* no. 24 (1983), p. 393.

9. Robert Brown, "On the Vegetable Products Used by American Indians," *Transactions of the Botanical Society,* vol. 9 (Edinburgh: Machlachlan, Stewart, and Company, 1868), p. 393.

10. L. S. Curtin, 1957 "Some Plants Used by The Yuki Indians of Round Valley, Northern California," *Southwest Museum Leaflets,* no. 20 (1957), p. 273.

11. C. A. Weslager, *Magic Medicines of the Indians* (New York: New American Library, 1983), p. 98.

12. Weslager, *Magic Medicines,* p. 139.

13. James Smith, *An Account of the Remarkable Occurrences in the Life and Travels of Colonel James Smith* (Cincinnati: Robert Clarke and Co., 1868), pp. 22-23.

14. Edmund Carpenter and Royal B. Hassrick, "Some Notes on Arrow Poisoning among the Tribes of the Eastern Woodlands," *Proceedings of the Delaware County Institute of Science,* vol. 10, no. 2 (1947), p. 49.

15. Wayne P. Suttles, *Coast Salish and Western Washington Indians.* Part 1 (New York: Garland, 1974), p. 322.

16. Marie Lucille Rocca-Arvay, "Assimilation and Resistance of the Yaqui Indians of Northern Mexico during the Colonial Period," Ph.D. dissertation. Columbia University, 1981, p. 120.

17. Theodore P. Banks, "Botanical and Ethnobotanical Studies of the Aleutian Islands," *Papers of the Michigan Academy of Sciences, Arts, and Letters,* vol. 37 (1951), p. 428.

18. Edward Arber, ed., *Travels and Works of Captain John Smith: President of Virginia and Admiral of New England: 1580-1631* (Edinburgh: John Grant, 1910), p. 62.

19. John Brickell, *The Natural History of North Carolina* (New York: Johnson Reprint Corporation, [1737] 1969), p. 351.

20. Huron H. Smith, "Ethnobotany of the Menomini Indians," *Bulletin of the Public Museum of the City of Milwaukee,* vol. 4, no. 3 (1923), p. 39.

21. Smith, "Ethnobotany of the Menomini Indians," pp. 40-41.

22. Leland Wyman and Stuart K. Harris, "The Ethnobotany of the Kayenta Navaho," *University of New Mexico Publications in Biology,* no. 5 (1951), p. 59.

Chapter Six: Paleo-Indian Poison Use

1. A good background on various issues concerning the Paleo-Indians may be found in almost any of Frison's works on the High Plains. See, for example, G. C. Frison and B. A. Bradley, *Folsom Tools and Technology at the Hanson Site, Wyoming* (Albuquerque: University of New Mexico Press, 1980), and G. C. Frison and E. Stanford, eds., *The Agate Basin Site: A Record of the Paleo-Indian Occupation of the Northwestern Plains* (New York: Academic Press, 1986). Jesse D. Jennings, *Prehistory of North America* (New York: McGraw-Hill, 1968), and Brian M. Fagan, *Ancient North America,* 3rd ed. (New York: Thames and Hudson, 2000), are classic texts on North American prehistory and provide a wide-ranging and current text and bibliography with which the interested reader may delve further into the topic.

2. Maureen L. King and Sergei B. Slobodin, "A Fluted Point from the Uptar Site, Northeastern Siberia," *Science,* vol. 2 (August 1996), pp. 634–66.

3. Gary Haynes and B. Sunday Eiselt, "The Power of Pleistocene Hunters-Gatherers: A Forward and Backward Search for Evidence about Mammoth Extinction," presented at symposium "Clovis and Beyond," Santa Fe, New Mexico, 1999, p. 2.

4. Haynes and Eiselt, "Power of Pleistocene Hunters-Gatherers," p. 2.

Conclusion

1. Robert Brown, "On the Vegetable Products Used by American Indians," *Transactions of the Botanical Society,* vol. 9 (Edinburgh: Machlachlan, Stewart, and Company, 1868), p. 387.

2. J. H. Hill, "Notes on Arrow Wounds," *American Journal of the Medical Sciences* (1862), p. 68.

3. Hill, "Notes on Arrow Wounds," p. 56.

4. Charles Hudson, *Knights of Spain, Warriors of the Sun* (Athens: University of Georgia Press, 1997), p. 244.

5. Adele Westbrook and Oscar Ratti, *Secrets of the Samurai* (Rutland, Vt.: Charles E. Tuttle, 1973), p. 238.

6. Henry M. Parrish, *Poisonous Snakebites in the United States* (New York: Vantage Press, 1980), p. 388.

7. Sherman A. Minton and Madge Rutherford Minton, *Venomous Reptiles* (New York: Charles Scribner's Sons, 1969), p. 121.

8. Henrietta H. Stockel, *The Lightning Stick: Arrows, Wounds, and Indian Legends* (Reno: University of Nevada Press, 1995), p. xiv.

9. Stockel, *Lightning Stick,* p. 16.

10. Linda B. King, "Medea Creek Cemetery: Late Inland Chumash Patterns of Social Organization, Exchange, and Warfare," Ph.D. dissertation, University of California, Los Angeles, 1982, p. 153.

11. A. J. Sowell, *Early Settlers and Indian Fighters of Southwest Texas* (Austin, Texas: State House Press, 1985), p. 400.

12. Sowell, *Early Settlers and Indian Fighters,* p. 648.

13. Stockel, *Lightning Stick,* p. xiv.

14. David E. Jones, *Native North American Armor, Shields, and Fortifications* (Austin: University of Texas Press, 2004).

15. Steven A. LeBlanc, *Prehistoric Warfare in the American Southwest* (Salt Lake City: University of Utah Press, 1990), p. 40.

Bibliography

Abraham, R. C. 1933. *The Tiv Peoples*. Lagos: Government Printer.

Arber, Edward, ed. 1910. *Travels and Works of Captain John Smith: President of Virginia and Admiral of New England: 1580–1631*. Edinburgh: John Grant.

Austin, Daniel F. 1980. "Historically Important Plants of Southeastern Florida." *Florida Anthropologist*. Vol. 33, no. 1.

Baker, Marc Andre. 1981. "The Ethnobotany of The Yurok, Tolowa, and Karok Indians of Northwestern California." Master's thesis, Humboldt State University.

Balick, M. Cox. 1996. *Plants, People, and Culture: The Science of Ethnobotany*. New York: Scientific American Library.

Banks, Theodore P. 1951. "Botanical and Ethnobotanical Studies of the Aleutian Islands." *Papers of the Michigan Academy of Sciences, Arts, and Letters*. Vol. 37.

Banks, William H. 1953. "Ethnobotany of the Cherokee Indians." Master's thesis, University of Tennessee.

Basso, Keith H., ed. 1971. *Western Apache Raiding and Warfare (From the Notes of Grenville Goodwin)*. Tucson: University of Arizona Press.

Batchelor, John. 1892. *The Ainu of Japan*. London: Religious Tract Society.

Beals, Ralph L. 1934. *Ethnology of the Nisenan*. University of California Publications in American Archaeology and Ethnology. Vol. 1.

Bean, Lowell J. 1990. "Gabrielino." In *Handbook of North American Indians*. Vol. 8. William C. Sturtevant, ed. Washington, D.C.: Smithsonian Institution.

Bean, Lowell J., and Katherine S. Saubel. 1972. *Temalpakh: Cahuilla Indian Knowledge and Usage of Plants*. Banning, Calif.: Malki Museum Press.

Black, Meredith J. 1980. *Algonquin Ethnobotany: An Interpretation of Aboriginal Adaptations in Southwestern Quebec*. Canadian Ethnology Service Papers no. 65. Ottawa: National Museum of Canada.

Blankinship, J. W. 1905. "Native Economic Plants of Montana." *Montana Agricultural College Experimental Station, Bulletin.* No. 56.

Bocek, Barbara R. 1967. "Ethnobotany of Costanoan Indians, California. Based on Collections by John P. Harrington." *Economic Botany.* Vol. 34, no. 2.

Bourke, John G. 1891. "Remarks on Arrows and Arrow Makers." *American Anthropologist.* Vol. 4, no.1.

Brickell, John. (1737) 1969. *The Natural History of North Carolina.* New York: Johnson Reprint Corporation.

Brown, Robert. 1868. "On the Vegetable Products Used by American Indians." *Transactions of the Botanical Society.* Vol. 9. Edinburgh: Machlachlan, Stewart, and Company.

Brugge, David M. 1961. "History, Huki, and Warfare: Some Random Data on The Lower Pima." *The Kiva.* Vol. 26, issue 4.

Burke, Edmund. 1957. *The History of Archery.* New York: William Morrow.

Burns, Alan. 1969. *History of Nigeria.* London: George Allen and Unwin.

Buskirk, Winfred. 1986. *The Western Apache.* Norman: University of Oklahoma Press.

Carpenter, Edmund and Royal B. Hassrick. 1957. "Some Notes on Arrow Poisoning Among the Tribes of the Eastern Woodlands." *Proceedings of the Delaware County Institute of Science.* Vol. 21.

Castaneda, Pedro. 1966. *The Journey of Coronado.* Ann Arbor, Mich.: University Microfilms.

Chamberlin, Ralph V. 1974. "The Ethnobotany of The Gosiute Indians of Utah." *Papers of the American Anthropological Association.* Part 5.

Chavannes, Edouard. trans. 1895–1905. *Les memoires historiques de Se-ma Ts'ien.* 5 vols. Maisonneuve: Pais.

Chestnut, V. K. 1974. *Plants Used by Indians of Mendocino County, California.* Willitis, Calif.: Mendocino County Historical Society.

Compton, Brian D. 1993. "Upper North Wakashan and Southern Tsimshian Ethnobotany: The Knowledge and Usage of Plants and Fungi Among the Oweekeno, Hanaksiala, Haisla, and Kitasoo Peoples of the Central and North Coast of British Columbia." Ph.D. dissertation, University of British Columbia.

Converse, H. M. 1908. "Myths and Legends of the Iroquois." *New York State Museum Bulletin.* No. 125.

Coon, Carleton S. 1970. *The Hunting Peoples.* Boston: Little, Brown.

Culley, John. 1936. "The California Indians: Their Medical Practices and Their Drugs." *Journal of the American Pharmaceutical Association*. Vol. 25, no. 4.

Curtin, L. S. 1957. "Some Plants Used by The Yuki Indians of Round Valley, Northern California." *Southwest Museum Leaflets*. No. 20.

Cusick, David. 1848. *Ancient History of The Six Nations*. Lockport, N.Y.: Turner and McCollum.

Densmore, Frances. 1926. "Uses of Plants by the Chippewa Indians." *Forty-Fourth Annual Report of the Bureau of American Ethnology to the Secretary of the Smithsonian Institution*. Washington, D.C.: Smithsonian Institution.

Dictionary of Daily Life of Indians of the Americas. Vol. 2. 1981. Newport Beach, Calif.: Publishers Incorporated.

Duff, Wilson. 1952. "The Upper Stalo Indians of the Fraser Valley, British Columbia." *Anthropology in British Columbia, Memoir*. No. 1.

Duke, James A. 1986. *Handbook of Northeastern Indian Medicinal Plants*. Lincoln, Mass.: Quarterman Publications.

Eldridge, S. 1897. "On the Arrow Poisons in Use among Ainos of Yeo." *Transactions of the Asiatic Society*. Vol. 4.

Elmore, Francis H. 1944. *Ethnobotany of the Navaho*. Albuquerque: University of New Mexico Press.

Fagan, Brian M. 2000. *Ancient North America*, 3rd. ed. New York: Thames and Hudson.

Felger, Richard S., and Mark Beck Moser. 1985. *People of The Desert and Sea*. Tucson: University of Arizona Press.

Feng, D. R., and L. G. Kilborn. 1937. "Nosu and Miao Arrow Poisons." *Journal of the West China Border Research Society*. Vol. 9.

Fenton, W. N. 1947. "An Early Cherokee Ethnobotanical Note." *Journal of the Washington Academy of Science*. Vol. 37, no. 3.

Flannery, Regina. 1939. "An Analysis of Coastal Algonquin Culture." *Catholic University of America, Anthropological Series*. No. 7.

Fletcher, Alice C., and Francis L. Flesche. 1972. *Omaha Tribe*. Vol. 2. Lincoln: University of Nebraska Press.

Fraser, Thomas R. 1916. "The Poisoned Arrows of the Abors and Mishmis of North-Eastern India and the Composition of Their Poisons." *Transactions of the Royal Society of Edinburgh*. Vol. 50.

Frison, G. C., and B. A. Bradley. 1980. *Folsom Tools and Technology at the Hanson Site, Wyoming*. Albuquerque: University of New Mexico Press.

Frison, G. C., and E. Stanford, eds. 1986. *Agate Basin Site: A Record of the Paleo-Indian Occupation of the Northwestern Plains.* New York: Academic Press.

Gibson, Emmett F. 1942. "Flipinos Blast Jap Chutists." *Chicago Herald-American.* July.

Gifford, E. W. 1950. "Atsugewi Ethnology." *University of California Publications. Anthropological Records.* Vol. 14.

————. 1930. "The Southern Yavapai." *University of California Publications in American Archaeology and Ethnology.* Vol. 29.

Gilmore, M. R. 1919. "Uses of Plants by Indians of the Missouri River Region." *Thirty-Third Annual Report of the Bureau of American Ethnology.* Washington, D.C.: Smithsonian Institution.

Goddard, Pliny Earle. 1903. "Life and Culture of The Hupa." *University of California Publications in American Archaeology and Ethnology.* Vol. 1, no. 1.

Goodrich, Jennie. 1980. *Kashaya Pomo Plants.* Los Angeles: American Indian Studies Center, University of California, Los Angeles.

Hamel, Paul B., and Mary U. Chiltoskey. 1972. *Cherokee Plants and Their Uses: A 400-Year History.* Sylva, N.C.: Herald Publishing.

Hamilton, Frances. 1824. "An Account of a Genus including the Herba Toxicaria of the Himalayan Mountains; Or, the Plant with Which the Natives Poison Their Arrows." *Edinburgh Journal of Science.* Vol. 2.

Hanson, C. 1967. "The Deadly Arrow." *Museum of the Fur Trade Quarterly.* Vol. 3, no. 4.

Hart, Jeffrey. 1981. "The Ethnobotany of The Northern Cheyenne." *Journal of Ethnopharmacology.* Vol. 4.

Haynes, Gary, and B. Sunday Eiselt. 1999. "The Power of Pleistocene Hunters-Gatherers: A Forward and Backward Search for Evidence about Mammoth Extinction." Presented at symposium "Clovis and Beyond," Santa Fe, New Mexico.

Heizer, Robert F. 1938. "Aconite Arrow Poison in the Old and New World." *Journal of the Washington Academy of Sciences.* Vol. 28.

————. 1938. "Aconite Poison Whaling in Asia and America: An Aleutian Transfer to the New World." *Smithsonian Institution, Bureau of American Ethnology Bulletin.* Vol. 133, no. 24.

Heizer, Robert F., and Albert B. Elsasser. 1980. *Natural World of the California Indians.* Los Angeles: University of California Press.

Heller, Christine A. 1953. *Edible and Poisonous Plants of Alaska.* College, Alaska: Cooperative Extension Service in Agriculture and Home Economics.

Herrick, James. 1995. *Iroquois Medical Botany*. Syracuse, N.Y.: Syracuse University Press.

Hill, J. H. 1862. "Notes on Arrow Wounds." *American Journal of The Medical Sciences*.

Hill, W. W. 1936. "Navaho Warfare." *Yale University Publications in Anthropology*. No. 5.

Hodge, Frederick Webb. 1910. *Handbook of American Indians North of Mexico*. Part 2. Smithsonian Institution, Bureau of America Ethnology, Bulletin 30. Washington, D.C.: Government Printing Office.

Hoffman, W. J. 1918. "Poisoned Arrows." *American Anthropologist*. Vol. 4.

Horton, James A. 1868. *West African Countries and Peoples*. Edinburgh: University Press.

Hudson, Charles. 1997. *Knights of Spain, Warriors of the Sun*. Athens: University of Georgia Press.

Jenness, Diamond A. 1980. "Algonquin Ethnobotany: An Interpretation of Aboriginal Adaptation in Southwestern Quebec." Canadian Ethnology Service, paper no. 65. Ottawa, Ontario.

Jennings, Jesse D. 1968. *Prehistory of North America*. New York: McGraw-Hill.

Johnson, Roy. 1967. *The Tuscaroras*. Murfreesboro, N.C.: Johnson Publishing.

Johnston, Alex. 1987. "Plants and the Blackfoot." *Lethbridge Historical Society: Occasional Papers*. No. 15.

Jones, Charles C. 1999. *Antiquities of the Southern Indians, Particularly of the Georgia Tribes*. Tuscaloosa: University of Alabama Press.

Jones, David E. 2004. *Native North American Armor, Shields, and Fortifications*. Austin: University of Texas Press.

Kelly, Isabel T. 1934. *Ethnobotany of the Surprise Valley Paiute*. University of California Publications in American Archeology and Ethnology. Vol. 31. Berkeley, Calif.

King, Linda B. 1982. "Medea Creek Cemetery: Late Inland Chumash Patterns of Social Organization, Exchange, and Warfare." Ph.D. dissertation, University of California, Los Angeles.

King, Maureen L., and Sergei B. Slobodin. 1996. "A Fluted Point From the Uptar Site, Northeastern Siberia." *Science*. 2 (August).

Kinielz, W. Vernon. 1940. *The Indians of the Western Great Lakes, 1615– 1760*. Ann Arbor: University of Michigan Press.

Kroeber, Clifton B., and Bernard L. Fontana. 1986. *Massacre on the Gila: An Account of the Last Major Battle between American Indians with Reflections on the Origin of War.* Tucson: University of Arizona Press.

Kuhm, Herbert. 1961. "Uses of Native Herbs by Wisconsin Indians." *Wisconsin Archaeologist.* Vol. 42, no. 3.

LeBlanc, Steven A. 1990. *Prehistoric Warfare in the American Southwest.* Salt Lake City: University of Utah Press.

Leiberg, John B. 1897. "General Report on a Botanical Survey of the Coeur D'Alene Mountains in Idaho during the Summer of 1895." *U.S. Department of Agriculture: Division of Botany.* Vol. 5, no. 1.

Lloyd, J. U., and C. G. Lloyd. 1884. *Drugs and Medicines of North America.* Cincinnati: J. U. Lloyd and C. G. Lloyd.

Longman, C. J., and W. Walrond. 1894. *Archery.* London: Longman, Green.

Lowie, Robert H. 1909. "The Northern Shoshone." *Anthropological Papers of the American Museum of Natural History.* Vol. 3, pt. 2.

Lynch, Kathleen. 1977. *Dena'ina K'etuna: Taniana Plantlore.* Anchorage, Alaska: Adult Literacy Laboratory, Anchorage Community College.

Mahar, James M. 1953. "Ethnobotany of the Oregon Paiutes of the Warm Springs Indian Reservation." Ph.D. dissertation, Reed College.

Mandelbaum, David G. 1979. *The Plains Cree: An Ethnographical, Historical, and Comparative Study.* Canadian Research Center, University of Regina. Regina, Saskatchewan.

Marles, Robin J., and J. Christina Clavelle. 2000. *Aboriginal Plant Use in Canada's Northwest Boreal Forests.* Vancouver: University of British Columbia Press.

Mayor, Adrienne. 2003. *Greek Fire, Poison Arrows, and Scorpion Bombs: Biological and Chemical Warfare in the Ancient World.* New York: Overlook Duckworth Publications.

————. 1997. "Dirty Tricks in Ancient Warfare." *Quarterly Journal of Military History.* Vol. 30, no. 2.

Meyer, Carl. 1971. "The Yurok of Trinidad Bay, 1851." In *The California Indians: A Source Book.* R. F. Heizer and M. A. Whipple, eds. Berkeley: University of California Press.

Minton, Sherman A., and Madge Rutherford Minton. 1969. *Venomous Reptiles.* New York: Charles Scribner's Sons.

Moerman, Daniel E. 1998. *Native American Ethnobotany.* Portland, Ore.: Timber Press.

Mozai, Torao. 1982. "Kublai's Khan's Lost Fleet." *National Geographic.* Vol. 162, no. 5.

Munson, Patrick. 1981. "Contributions to Osage and Lakota Ethnobotany." *Plains Anthropologist.* Vol. 26, no. 93.

Murphey, Edith V. A. 1958. *Indian Uses of Native Plants.* Glenwood, Ill.: Myerbooks.

Newcomb, W. W. 1974. *The Indians of Texas.* Austin: University of Texas Press.

Olmsted, D. L., and Omer C. Stewart. 1990. "Achumawi." In *Handbook of North American Indians.* Vol. 8. William C. Sturtevant, ed. Washington, D.C.: Smithsonian Institution.

Opler, Morris. 1944. *Chiricahua Apache Material Relating to Sorcery.* Washington, D.C.: Catholic University of America Press.

Parrish, Henry M. 1980. *Poisonous Snakebites in the United States.* New York: Vantage Press.

Paxman, J., and R. Harris. 1982. *A Higher Form of Killing: The Secret Story of Chemical and Biological Warfare.* New York: Hill and Wang.

Peacock, Sandra Leslie. 1968. "Piikani Ethnobotany: The Traditional Plant Knowledge of the Piikani Peoples of the Northwestern Plains." Master's thesis, University of Calgary.

Porsild, A. E. 1953. "Edible Plants of the Arctic." *Calgary Arctic Institute of North America.* Vol. 6.

Powers, S. 1873. "Aboriginal Botany." *Proceedings of the California Academy of Science.* Vol. 5. Berkeley: University of California.

Pursh, Frederick. 1868. *Botanical Excursion in the Northeastern Parts of the States of Pennsylvania and New York during the Year 1807.* Onondaga: Onondaga Historical Association.

Reeves, Carolyn Keller. 1985. *The Choctaw before Removal.* Jackson: University Press of Mississippi.

Ricciuti, Edward R. 1978. *The Devil's Garden: Facts and Folklore of Perilous Plants.* New York: Walker and Company.

Rocca-Arvay, Marie Lucille. 1981. "Assimilation and Resistance of the Yaqui Indians of Northern Mexico during the Colonial Period." Ph.D. dissertation, Columbia University.

Romero, John B. 1954. *The Botanical Lore of The California Indians.* New York: Vantage Press.

Roth, H. Ling. 1966. *Great Benin: Its Customs, Art, and Horrors.* New York: Barnes and Noble.

Safford, W. E. 1916. "Narcotic Plants and Stimulants of the Ancient
    Americans." *Annual Report of the Smithsonian Institution*. Wash-
    ington, D.C.: Smithsonian Institution.
Sagard, Father, and W. N. Fenton. [1630] 1947. "Early Cherokee Eth-
    nobotanical Note." *Journal of the Washington Academy of Science*.
    Vol. 37, no. 3.
Sauer, Martin. 1802. *An Account of a Geographical and Astronomical Expe-
    dition to the North Parts of Russia Performed by Commodore Joseph
    Billings: 1785–1794*. London: A. Strahan.
Saunders, Charles F. 1920. *Edible and Useful Wild Plants of the United
    States and Canada*. New York: Dover.
Schenck, Sara M., and E. W. Gifford. 1952. "Karok Ethnobotany."
    Anthropological Records. Vol. 13, no. 6.
Sharpe, J., and T. B. Underwood. 1973. *American Indian Cooking and
    Herb Lore*. Cherokee, N.C.: Cherokee Publications.
Smart, Jeffery K. 1997. *Textbook of Military Medicine: Medicinal Aspects
    of Chemical and Biological Warfare*. Aberdeen, Md.: U.S. Army
    Chemical and Biological Defense Command, Aberdeen Prov-
    ing Grounds.
Smith, Huron H. 1923. "Ethnobotany of the Menomini Indians." *Bul-
    letin of the Public Museum of the City of Milwaukee*. Vol. 4, no. 3.
———. 1922. "Ethnobotany of the Ojibwe Indians." *Bulletin of the
    Public Museum of the City of Milwaukee*. Vol. 4, no. 3.
Smith, James. 1868. *An Account of The Remarkable Occurrences in the Life
    and Travels of Colonel James Smith*. Cincinnati: Robert Clarke
    and Co.
Sowell, A. J. 1985. *Early Settlers and Indian Fighters of Southwest Texas*.
    Austin, Texas: State House Press.
Speck, Frank G. 1937. "Catawba Herbal and Curative Practices." *Jour-
    nal of American Folklore*. Vol. 57.
———. 1928. "Chapters on The Ethnology of the Powhatan Tribes
    of Virginia." *Museum of the American Indian. Heye Foundation:
    Indian Notes*. Vol. 1, no. 5.
Spier, Leslie. 1928. "Havasupai Ethnography." *Anthropological Papers of
    the American Museum of Natural History*. Vol. 29, pt. 3.
Spring, Christopher. 1993. *African Arms and Armor*. Washington, D.C.:
    Smithsonian Institution Press.
Stern, Theodore. 1990. "Klamath and Modoc." In *Handbook of North
    American Indians*. Vol. 12. William C. Sturtevant, ed. Washing-
    ton, D.C.: Smithsonian Institution.

Stockel, Henrietta H. 1995. *The Lightning Stick: Arrows, Wounds, and Indian Legends*. Reno: University of Nevada Press.

Strike, Sandra S. 1994. *Ethnobotany of the California Indians*. Vol. 2: *Aboriginal Uses of California's Indigenous Plants*. Königstein, Germany: Koeltz Scientific Books.

Suttles, Wayne P. 1974. *Coast Salish and Western Washington Indians*. Part 1. New York: Garland.

Swanton, John. 1924. "Aboriginal Culture of The Southeast." *Forty-Second Annual Report of The Bureau of American Ethnology to the Secretary of the Smithsonian Institution*. Washington, D.C.: Smithsonian Institution.

———. 1922. "Early History of the Creek Indians and Their Neighbors." *Bulletin of the Bureau of American Ethnology*. Vol. 73.

Tantaquidgeon, Gladys. 1972. "Folk Medicine of The Delaware and Related Algonquian Indians." *Pennsylvania Historical Museum Commission Anthropological Series*. No. 3.

Taylor, Lyda Averill. 1940. *Plants Used as Curatives by Certain Southeastern Tribes*. Cambridge, Mass.: Botanical Museum of Harvard University.

Teit, James. 1900. "The Lillooet Indians." *Memoir of the American Museum of Natural History*. Vol. 3.

———. 1900. "The Thompson Indians of British Columbia." *Memoir of the American Museum of Natural History*. Vol. 2.

Timbrook, Jan. 1990. "Ethnobotany of the Chumash Indians. California. Based on Collections by John P. Harrington." *Economic Botany*. Vol. 44, no. 2.

Townsend, J. B. 1983. "Firearms against Native Arms." *Arctic Anthropology*. Vol. 20, no. 2.

Turner, Nancy J. 1997. *Food Plants of Interior First Peoples*. Vancouver: University of British Columbia Press.

———. 1995. *Food Plants of Coastal First Peoples*. Vancouver: University of British Columbia Press.

———. 1983. "Ethnobotany of the Nitinaht Indians of Vancouver Island." *British Columbia Provincial Museum*. No. 24.

———. 1980. "Ethnobotany of the Okanagan-Colville Indians of British Columbia and Washington." *Occasional Papers of the British Columbia Provincial Museum*. No. 21.

———. 1973. "The Ethnobotany of the Bella Coola Indians of British Columbia." *Syesis: Provincial Museum of British Columbia*. Vol. 6.

Vestal, Paul A. 1944. "Ethnobotany of the Ramah Navaho." *Papers of the Peabody Museum of American Archaeology and Ethnology: Howard University.* Vol. 60, no. 4.

Voegelin, Erminie W. 1938. "Tubatulabal Ethnography." *University of California Anthropological Records.* Vol. 2, no. 1.

Vogel, Virgil J. 1949. *American Indian Medicine.* Norman: University of Oklahoma Press.

Wallace, William J. 1949. "Hupa Warfare." *Masterkey.* Vol. 23.

Wallis, Wilson D., and Ruth Sawtell Wallis. 1952. *The Micmac Indians of Eastern Canada.* Minneapolis: University of Minnesota Press.

Warren, William W. 1984. *History of the Ojibway People.* St. Paul: Minnesota Historical Society.

Weiner, Michael A. 1972. *Earth Medicines—Earth Foods.* New York: Collier Books.

Weslager, C. A. 1983. *Magic Medicines of the Indians.* New York: New American Library.

Westbrook, Adele, and Oscar Ratti. 1973. *Secrets of The Samurai.* Rutland, Vt.: Charles E. Tuttle.

Witthoft, J. 1954. "An Early Cherokee Ethnobotanical Note." *Washington Academy of Sciences.* Vol. 37.

Worcester, D. E. 1945. "The Weapons of American Indians," *New Mexico Historical Review.* Vol. 20, no. 8.

Wyman, Leland, and Stuart K. Harris. 1951. "The Ethnobotany of the Kayenta Navaho." *University of New Mexico Publications in Biology.* No. 5.

Zigmond, Maurice L. 1981. *Kawaiisu Ethnobotany.* Salt Lake City: University of Utah Press.

Index